1Question

That Can Change Your Life!

*Unleash The Power of Your Self-Worth
To Secure Success, Happiness, Love,
And Fulfillment In Your Life*

MONIKA LASCHKOLNIG

Illustrated by
MARGRET ZITTERBAYER

STERLING PUBLISHING GROUP
www.SterlingPublishingGroup.com

PRAISE FOR
1 QUESTION THAT CAN
CHANGE YOUR LIFE

"1 Question That Can Change Your Life" connects your sense of self-worth to your self-esteem and your success in life. It's a practical guide, enabling you to go deep within in an easy way and find out what you are worthy of. So accept the invitation and get ready for transformation."

~ Jack Canfield, Co-author, *Chicken Soup for the Soul* and Co-founder, National Association of Self-Esteem (USA)

"This book takes the reader quickly to the most profound and essential awareness—that of genuine self-love. Read this book today to wake to heart of the matter in your life and start living with the peace and joy you deserve."

~ Sonia Choquette
  NY Times best-selling author of *The Answer Is Simple*

"A simplistically brilliant read that taught me some powerful things about myself and my relationship to others. Buy this book! It is wonderful."

~ Teresa de Grosbois, President, Wildfire Workshops Inc.

PRAISE FOR
1 QUESTION THAT CAN
CHANGE YOUR LIFE

"Monika Laschkolnig gently and compassionately guides readers through an exciting journey back to their inherent sense of worthiness. If everyone on the planet were to embrace their personal worthiness, there'd be significantly fewer emotional troubles, divorces and wars."

~ Deborah Sandella, Ph.D.
  Psychotherapist and author of the award-winning book
  Releasing The Inner Magician

"The book is very good—I thoroughly enjoyed it. It is written in a way that you think it is being read to you personally."

~ Janet Powers, Chief Executive Diva, Diva Toolbox™, LLC

"This exciting book offers a practical and effective process for transforming one's life in the areas of work, love, family life, health and lifestyle. It is based on sound research, yet presented in a manner that makes it easy to understand and apply. It has the power to make a significant difference in individuals, families and the world."

~ Robert Reasoner, Past President
  International Council for Self-Esteem

1 QUESTION THAT CAN CHANGE YOUR LIFE - *Unleash The Power of Your Self-Worth To Secure Success, Happiness, Love and Fulfillment In Your Life*

This is a work of non-fiction. This publication is designed to provide accurate information on the subject matter covered. It is sold with the understanding that the publisher is not engaged in rendering professional services or advice. The information is not intended to replace any legal council or other professional directives. If professional services or advice or other assistance is required, the services of a professional should be sought.

ISBN: 978-0-9845010-6-9

Library of Congress Control: On File With The Publisher

Published by The Sterling Publishing Group, USA 1.888.689.1130
www.SterlingPublishingGroup.com

Printed in the United States of America

Editor, Cover Design & Layout: Jodi Nicholson www.jodinicholson.com
Illustrator: Margret Zitterbayer

This book may be ordered through the publisher or online from the author at: www.WhatAreYouWorthyOf.com

Self-Help / Personal Growth
Self-Esteem

DEDICATION

I dedicate this book with heart-felt thanks
to my amazing teacher, Sonia Choquette
who helped me to reconnect with
the light of my spirit;

to my mentor and friend, Lauri DeJulian
who prepared me for this way helping me to
embrace and remove my shadows;

and to my spirit playfully opening possibilities
I didn't even imagine were there.

ACKNOWLEDGMENTS

This book has come into being thanks to an ongoing support and encouragement of many friends who believed in me, and saw the benefit for the world to learn how to unfold the power of self-worth through "The 1 Question Process". I am deeply grateful and give many thanks to all of you!

To my amazing teacher Sonia Choquette—thank you for all your love, for mirroring the value of my work back to me, and for your encouragement to take that one question and make it into a book. You are the godmother of this project as your believing in me made me a writer. But first of all, you helped me connect with the inner voice of my spirit, which I am eternally thankful for.

To my mentor and dearest friend Lauri DeJulian—thank you for patiently guiding me out of the valley of shadows into the Light in your amazing non-judgmental, loving, and caring way; I am eternally thankful for your deepest insights, unshaken trust and every conversation we had.

To the President and Founder of the National (US) and International Council For Self-Esteem, Robert Reasoner, and a respected friend—we were privileged to accompany you on your educational travels across Europe and got impressed by your tireless devotion in spreading the awareness of the crucial role of self-esteem for the individual and its impact on the whole society.

To my powerful success coach, Jack Canfield—thank you for your continuous focus on enhancing self-worth and self-esteem throughout all your seminars as there is no success without them. Your business trainings were always not only highly professional but also very inspiring, as they included the holistic approach of body, spirit and mind. They changed my approach to life and business.

To my friend and a great artist, Margret Zitterbayer—thank you for seeing the value of this book long before it was ready, and illustrating it so beautifully. Thank you for all the love you put into painting the "You Are Worthy" card deck accompanying the book.

To my friend, Leslie Gebhart—thank you for you patience and time you spent checking if my English sounds like "real street English". And thank you for cheering me on along the way.

To my book advisor Teresa de Grosbois at Wildfire Workshops Inc—thank you for giving me a profound know-how about all aspects of writing and publishing a book. Your coaching made me understand that being an author means nowadays so much more than just writing a book. Thank you for sharing this knowledge so generously.

To the heaven-sent Jodi Nicholson at Sterling Publishing Group—thank you for taking this project into the world with your highly professional approach, and in an ongoing atmosphere of kindness and support.

To my friend, Anna Höglinger—thank you for always being a sparkle of joy.

To my office manager, Sandra Gratz—thank you for doing your work so excellently that I had space of mind to take on a new project and write a book. You are a true treasure.

To my husband, Martin, and our two children Caroline and Kian—your love has changed my life.

TABLE OF CONTENTS

TABLE OF CONTENTS

1Question

That Can Change Your Life!

*Unleash The Power of Your Self-Worth
To Secure Success, Happiness, Love,
And Fulfillment In Your Life*

MONIKA LASCHKOLNIG

Illustrated by
MARGRET ZITTERBAYER

STERLING PUBLISHING GROUP
www.SterlingPublishingGroup.com

INTRODUCTION

My Wish For You ...

This book has been created in an atmosphere of ongoing support, love, seeing the best in another, encouragement, and friendship. I make a deep wish that taking it into your hands, you too shall feel this vibration.

May you attain peace in your life once you have recognized the beauty and dignity of your innate treasure of worthiness, which you have never lost, thus don't need to earn back—it's yours by birth. It's yours forever. And once you unleash the power of this realization, it will be able to transform your life into living your heart's desire, as you will understand the missing link to success.

May it lead you to a truly fulfilled life, bringing joy and peace into your world.

Monika Laschkolnig

CHAPTER 1

BORN, THUS WORTHY

You are worthy.

You are a worthy human being. There is no doubt about it. You are worthy because you exist. Your worthiness is your birthmark. Yours, his, hers, theirs... Ours. It is the birthmark of the human race. Thus to claim your worth is your birthright.

Everyone was born aware of his or her self-worth. Some grew up in surroundings where they could experience it every day. Some were less lucky and, as they were growing up, they started forgetting that they are worthy beings. Some listened to others' opinions and learned from them what to think about themselves. Now the time has come to rediscover the core of your being: your worthiness.

Knowing your worthiness is a part of knowing who you are. And why is it so important? My mentor and friend, Lauri DeJulian, told me once: "Know who you are, so you don't need someone else's definition of you to fill in your blanks."

It struck me—so simple and so powerful. Yet do you really know yourself or are you listening to how others define you? You so often give your power away to others by letting them evaluate you and decide for you who you are and what you are worthy of. You value their opinion more than your own feeling about yourself. It is time to change that and start owning the profound certainty of your authentic self. Do you know who you are beyond your name and social status? Are you aware how precious and unique you are? Not because of what you do but because you are. Yes, that simple—your existence is a gift. You exist endowed with your inner qualities, even if you are not conscious about your inner richness. No matter what you have been doing, what life you have led, or where you are standing now—be it the most wonderful or demanding place—your worth does not depend on it. You were born with a set of inner treasures—you might have forgotten or learned to ignore them, but stay assured that they are there and you can choose to go back to square one and start anew. It might be easy for some and more difficult for others, so don't compare yourself to anyone else, just allow yourself to follow your own unique way.

Even before you were officially given a name, you were already a worthy human being. But, are you fully aware of your worthiness?

Some people can easily list what they are worthy of: "I'm worthy of . . . and of . . . and of . . ." The majority, however, will not have an immediate answer; they will start pondering. "Yes, it feels somehow true . . . But what actually am I worthy of?"

Whether you can pronounce it straightaway or just have this veiled sense of worth and need some time to consider how to express it, each and every individual knows the answer; some consciously, and some have it hidden deep inside and need more time to reconnect with this inner knowing. Rest assured, even if you needed more time to find it out, it is alright because you have the time you need to find it out step by step.

This book is your "Hidden Treasure Map" which will lead you to discovering your inner richness, which, in turn, will lead to enhancing your self-esteem to make your life even better. It will also give you means to explore different aspects of your worthiness, and will explain how your success in all areas of life is linked to your self-worth and how you can unleash its potential to create more stability, security, happiness, love, and overall fulfillment in your life. This book is for you and about you, so it is going to be a fascinating exploration leading you to realizations regarding yourself that you haven't been aware of up to now. You will obtain some inner peace by realizing what a worthy being you are. So let the Story Of You unfold as you progress with the book.

Chapter 2

❧ · ❧

SELF-WORTH AND SELF-ESTEEM

What is self-esteem actually? Nathaniel Brandon, the pioneer in the field of self-esteem describes it as follows: *"Self-esteem is a disposition to experience oneself as being competent to cope with the basic challenges of life and of being worthy of happiness."*

There are two components of self-esteem: a feeling of self-worth and a feeling of competence. Thus a healthy self-esteem is much more than just feeling good.

Each of you is able to list examples of your competence: you have successfully learned to walk and speak (having a 2-year old at home, who gets frustrated not being able to express himself, although clearly knowing what he wants, reminds me constantly what a crucial competence speaking is!). You know how to eat with a knife and fork, and how to take care of yourself. You might have become skillful with some sort of discipline. Or you have finished school, learned a job, and graduated from a college or university. You might have become a skilled craftsman, an accomplished scientist or a successful mother — all possibilities bringing an equal sense of competence, though in different areas of life.

While building up your sense of competence, you were not necessarily building up your worthiness. You might have been born to a family fostering your sense of worthiness by creating a surrounding respecting child's worthiness right from the beginning. Or you have grown up in less favorable circumstances, forgetting more and more what you are worthy of. It could have also been that your accomplishments were valued more than you as a person. In either case, you have never lost your worthiness! Whether you are an optimist or a pessimist, an extrovert or an introvert, no matter what you have accomplished or how many failures you have experienced – everyone is equally worthy. You cannot be more or less worthy than anyone else. The same way every person is born with a navel, everyone is born knowing "I am worthy". Each navel looks slightly different, although it is the same thing; the same way people may feel worthy of different aspects of life, although every individual without an exception has the same sense of self-worth.

I have observed a common pattern: There are a few aspects which every human being feels worthy of without an exception:

- Worthy of love
- Worthy of being themselves
- Worthy of experiencing happiness

While feeling worthy of something, you do not always feel that you deserve it. I will discuss this discrepancy later, for now, focusing solely on the self-worth as a building block of self-esteem.

No one can take the feeling of self-worth away from you and no one can give it to you; others may have trained you to neglect or forget it, but no one could have ever taken it away. That is excellent news because it means you still have it inside, no matter if accessible, veiled, or deeply hidden. This program will give you tools to look for, find, and bring your inner treasures to the surface of consciousness.

Perception of your self-worth and your competence is subjective and it is solely you who can enhance your own self-esteem. You can be given circumstances favorable for this process, but it is you and you only who can re-establish your own worthiness for yourself, so please take your time to go through this process step by step.

Healthy, authentic self-esteem is much more than just having positive feelings about your self, others and the world. Bob Reasoner (an educator and a founder of the National Association for Self-Esteem and the International Council of Self-Esteem) distinguishes four types of self-esteem.

**HIGH
SELF-WORTH**

Defensive Self-Esteem
(Type 1)

High Self-Esteem

**LOW
COMPETENCE** ———————————————— **HIGH
COMPETENCE**

Low Self-Esteem

Defensive Self-Esteem
(Type 2)

**LOW
SELF-WORTH**

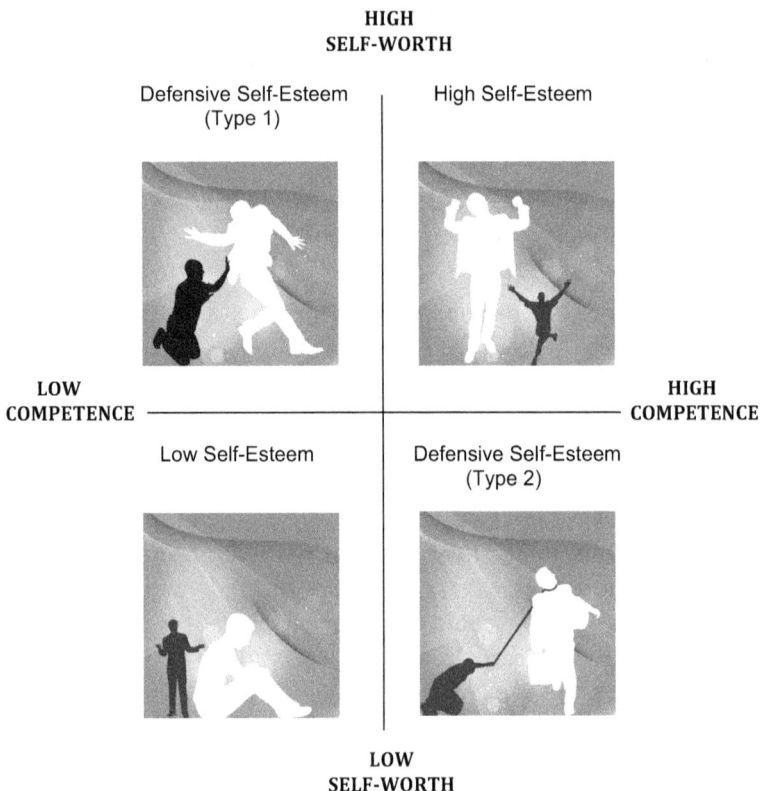

Self-esteem is a subjective matter: It is a sense of self-worth and a self-evaluation of one's own competence. It does not necessarily correspond to the worth or competence that the world assigns you. Thus your subjective perception of discrepancies between your inner estimation and the outer evaluation might result in the form of a defensive self-esteem.

Let's examine each of them separately.

1. High Self-Esteem Type:

Healthy feeling of self-worth and a high sense of competence

If you have high self-esteem, you feel able to cope with the basic challenges of life, you feel worthy of love, happiness, and being yourself. You know who you are and you do not need to prove anything to anyone. You are able to admit your mistakes and acknowledge others' achievements.

It might be a case that you have an overall good self-esteem, however there is an area of your life where you somehow notice a deficit. Therefore, I invite you as well to go on the exploration of your worth to see what puzzle piece is missing to make yourself complete.

2. Low Self-Esteem Type:

Low self-worth and low sense of competence

If you have low self-esteem, you feel overwhelmed with the basic challenges of life, you have a thought pattern, a belief, that you are unworthy of happiness or love and you don't value yourself and your achievements. You define who you are through others' opinions of you. You tend to filter the positive opinions of yourself out, as they seem too unrealistic because they do not resemble your set of beliefs about yourself.

It is difficult for you to admit your mistakes, which might result in telling lies. As you feel helpless and overwhelmed by the challenges your life constantly offers, you cannot easily acknowledge and rejoice in others' achievements—instead you might experience jealousy or envy.

Even if you have ended up in this tight spot called low self-esteem, I have got good news for you: it is not a dead-end street. You were born knowing that you are worthy. You have developed different types of competence one after the other. Already the fact that you are reading this book means that you have learned to read. Even before you started school, you had already developed a wide range of competence in different areas of life. It might have happened, however, that your environment set such high expectations that your newly acquired skills were not noticed and you have not learned to recognize and value your achievements. Or maybe your family members, teachers and other people in your life important to you were too preoccupied with their issues to pay attention to your development. Moreover, your environment probably did not show respect for you as a child, so as the time passed by, you have forgotten that you are worthy.

Instead of focusing on all that went wrong, I would like to encourage you to find the wealth you have got in yourself all the time. Even if it has managed to stay unnoticed for a while, everything is there! You might need to do some inner exploration before you find all the treasures, so I will do my best to approach it from different sides, to make it possible for you to make some discoveries that may turn out significant for your future.

3. Defensive Self-Esteem - Type 1:

High self-worth but low sense of competence

If you have this type of a defensive self-esteem, you feel subjectively that the world does not assign you with competence that would correspond with your self-worth feeling.

You constantly feel more competent than you think your family, friends, boss, co-workers, etc. would entrust you with. Their opinion of you makes you feel inadequate and, therefore, you constantly try to prove that you are more competent than they think you are. This might lead to a need of validating yourself through outer signs of achievement, such as various status symbols and a corresponding life-style, to make others believe you are already there, in hope that they will recognize your competence and will entrust you with tasks, responsibilities and recognition that you feel would correspond with your abilities and worth.

The feeling of inadequacy can also express itself as a drive to overachieve, compete and prove oneself in various situations. It can also express itself as an –ism state: perfectionism, workaholism, etc. You might have a tendency to show yourself as overeager to the person you would like to convince about your competence. You will probably feel inferior towards those who stand higher in the hierarchy and superior towards people who you feel are less competent than you, seeing however their achievements as a danger to your own position, thus not being able to acknowledge their success whole-heartedly.

This self-esteem type may manifest in children as a bully, i.e. establishing respect for one's competence by force. Another way of coping with the feeling of inadequacy is playing a "super-cool kid" who has got it all and expects to be respected for the skills usually associated with items they are showing off with.

Although your feeling of self-worth is relatively high, you may wish to change the perception of your competence. There might be some aspects of your self-worth which, when found and addressed, will allow you to acknowledge your competence in a natural way.

4. Defensive Self-Esteem - Type 2:

Low self-worth but high sense of competence

If you are endowed with this type of the defensive self-esteem, you feel that although the world respects you a lot and assigns you with high competence, you are unworthy of it. It results in a self-sabotaging behavior, literally suffocating your success.

The most illustrative examples are the prominent people who achieve a high status due to their competence within a relatively short time and at a certain moment the situation overwhelms them. The feeling that they are not worthy of such an attention and respect makes them subconsciously get into self-sabotaging behavior, such as alcohol excesses, getting caught while betraying their spouse, getting involved with scandals etc., just to prove "See, I'm not worth your high opinion of me." Their behavior results in a harsh critique that finally matches their low self-worth feeling.

It is not only people who have achieved a lot that have a problem caused by the discrepancy between how they feel about themselves and what the world thinks about them. Whenever the sense of competence rises significantly above the subjective feeling of self-worth in any of us, there is a high probability of ending up with some self-sabotage pattern. However, there is a possibility of preventing such an outcome by enhancing your feeling of self-worth.

When you examine the above model carefully, a certain pattern becomes vivid: It is the level of self-worth that dictates the behavior!

High self-worth in the Defensive Self-Esteem Type 1 tries to increase the feeling of competence, whereas low self-worth in the Type 2 causes a subconscious self-sabotaging behavior that damages the competence.

That shows us how crucial awareness of our self-worth is. The self-worth is the absolute basis of our healthy functioning as human beings, the foundation of a happy and fulfilled life. Only if you feel worthy of growing, expanding, learning etc., will you develop competence in a respective field. Competence is secondary to self-worth and can be acquired through learning, achieving, and accomplishing things. Self-worth cannot be learned or obtained —it is a knowing coming from within. The question is, are you aware you that you are endowed with it?

A solid feeling of self-worth is the basis for a healthy self-esteem. Sometimes people are concerned there might be danger of getting conceited, proud or arrogant as the result of achieving high self-esteem. I would like to dispel this misunderstanding: it is the self-confidence with a missing sense of self-worth that might lead to such a result. However, asking if you can get too much self-esteem is like asking: Can you get too healthy? Enhancing your feeling of self-worth and competence will lead to a healthy self-esteem, which is the foundation of a healthy, fulfilled and successful life.

We will soon embark on a journey in quest of your hidden treasures of various aspects of self-worth that you will find within yourself. If you had a diamond—would you rather keep it well hidden thriving on the knowledge you possess a treasure? Or would you use it as a piece of jewelry accompanying you in your life, using it and cherishing its beauty? Your self-worth is like a diamond. You can never lose it. However, in order to use it, you need to find it again, polish it clean and make it visible to yourself to fully realize all its beauty and value.

In order to find your path to the core of your being, I will keep asking you a question which will lead you to answers you might have already sensed inside, although the clarity could have been missing up to now.

No negative thought you have ever entertained had the power to change the truth of who you are. It might have obscured the pure view of your nature, but it is not able to forever veil the feeling that you are a worthy being because deep inside you have always known who you are.

You may be shy at the beginning to look at and acknowledge the unique person you are. So let's take one step at the time and begin with having a closer look at your worth.

CHAPTER 3

❧

DIAMOND OR GLASS?
WHAT SELF-WORTH AND SELF-ESTEEM
ARE OFTEN MISTAKEN FOR

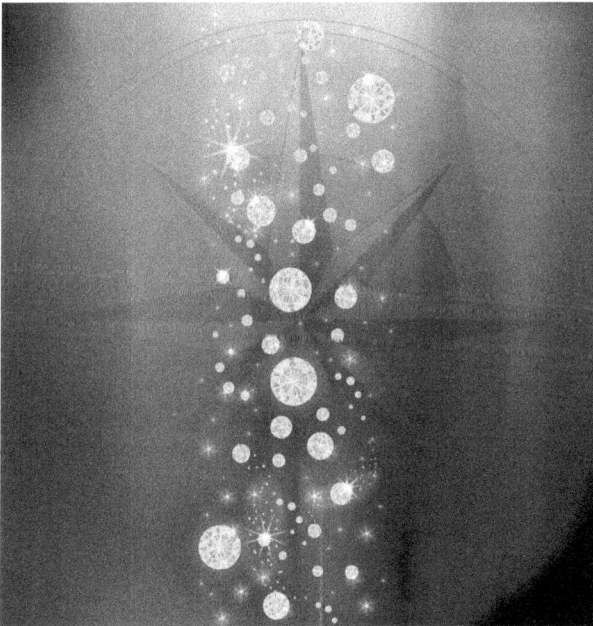

Self-esteem versus self-confidence

Self-esteem is a notion used by many nowadays, although some mistake it for self-confidence. There is a difference between these two concepts.

Self-esteem is a combination of self-worth and competence, whereas self-confidence means trust in one's own judgment, ability, power, etc. High self-esteem is the basis for self-confidence and it automatically results in self-confidence. A person with low self-esteem will lack self-confidence in most, if not all, areas of their life. The defensive types of self-esteem may result in an unbalanced self-confidence. An individual may develop 'too much' self-confidence expressed as superiority or arrogance while actually feeling incompetent or low self-worth.

"I'm worthy" versus "I deserve"

It is a commonplace to use the phrase "You deserve this" or "You don't deserve that". "Enjoy your holidays—you've been working so hard, so you really deserve it! ", "You are such a good girl, you deserve a caring husband", etc. Let's have a closer look at the difference between the meaning of "I deserve" and "I'm worthy of".

Have you ever noticed that the phrase "You deserve it" is much more frequently used when you talk to somebody while you usually think about yourself in negative terms: "I don't deserve it". For example, you would be ready to tell your friend "You deserve to be successful in business because you have been trying hard," at the same time thinking "I wouldn't deserve to earn that much money." It is another social convention. Once you have become aware of that, it will be easier for you to break free from thinking patterns that were passed on to you.

When you say "I deserve" you start from the position where you do not have something but hope that it may be granted to you if you are good enough, when you put some effort into gaining it, or if you behave properly.

When you say "I'm worthy of something", you feel it inside as the most natural characteristic of yourself as a human being without a need to prove anything to anyone — you just claim what is there for you by your birthright: love, respect, abundance, happiness, well-being and many other things you might feel worthy of.

The paradox is that some people feel worthy of love etc., but at the same time they feel they don't deserve it. That shows clearly that we know what we are worthy of but we have learned from our environment what we do and don't deserve. By being told what we deserve and when and how to get it, we were manipulated into behaviors established as a norm by the society that may not necessarily reflect our personal values. As individuals we often give in to the pressure of the so-called "social norm", suppressing and forgetting what we know for ourselves as true. What is the result? Frustration, feeling unfulfilled, giving oneself up for others, giving pieces of our soul away, the light in us fades away, we start feeling disconnected or, finally even "internally dead" living just by default. Habits that serve others and society take over and we forget to nurture the person whom we should take care of in the first place— ourselves.

When your knowing comes from within, you do not need any confirmation from outside. That's how you can discern between acquired "truths" and your authentic innate knowing. One of the unquestionable inner truths is: "I am worthy".

If anyone ever questions that, it is a sign they have forgotten the truth about themselves. As author and psychologist Marshall B.

Rosenberg suggested, "Analyses of others are actually expressions of our own needs and values"[1], so just focus on what you feel worthy of and not on what someone else might think you deserve.

CHAPTER 4

❦

THE QUESTION ...
WHAT ARE YOU WORTHY OF?

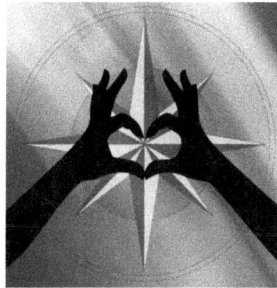

We all carry a distinct feeling of worthiness in us. We all know we are worthy beings. We also know what we are worthy of, though life circumstances might have lead us to have forgotten that.

When we slow down for a moment, and start listening to our inner voice, we will infallibly know that we are worthy; it is not a thought or an idea which we need first to develop to own, but it is an intrinsic concept embedded in each human being. Everyone without exception is able to reconnect with it.

You live your life in accordance with your belief of what you are worthy of. If you don't have a sense of worthiness, you don't feel worthy of developing competence or growing your skills. This results in low self-esteem and diminished possibility to develop your abilities because defensive mechanisms will be activated.

Being conscious of your worthiness creates the basis of healthy high self-esteem and allows you to recognize, acknowledge, and naturally respect others' self-worth. In this way, your presence will make a difference in others' lives.

Your worthiness is the basis of your happy and successful life. It is the essential building block of your healthy self-esteem that influences your self-confidence and allows you to have dreams. They, in turn, enable you to formulate your goals that you feel worthy of pursuing. In this way, you create a meaningful and fulfilling life.

If the foundation is not solid, even the most beautiful house built upon it, will not be stable. In the same way, only when you discover what you are worthy of and enhance your self-esteem, will you create a solid basis for your potential to unfold to its fullest. And that's the purpose of this process.

How can you benefit to the maximum from this program that can change your life?

You will be answering some questions when going through this transformational process. Please remember: there is no right or wrong answer. There is nothing to achieve here. There is nothing to prove to anyone. It is between you and you. This book is your workbook where you note down your innermost thoughts, feelings and ideas. They are all valid, they are all a part of your way, and they are all okay. There is no need to hide anything; but there is also no gain from exaggerating. Just always answer the first thing that comes to your mind. Do not hold back but do not force yourself to come up with an answer if you momentarily go blank. If you don't come up with all the answers, you can review the questions at a later point and write the answers down as they appear.

To get the most of out this process there is only one rule: Answer the questions honestly. And remember—you cannot fail or lose anything; on the contrary, with each answer, you get and reclaim yet another part of the precious you back.

The *"What Are You Worthy Of?"* transformational process consists of three steps, which are built upon each other:

1. In Step 1, you will start listening to your inner voice.

2. In Step 2, you will listen to your physical wisdom.

3. And in Step 3, you will look into some specific areas of your life.

Let's embark now on the journey inwards in quest of discovering what treasures are hidden inside.

STEP 1 – Your Inner Voice

We will begin with a general question—each time you answer, write down the first thing that comes to your mind. Please remember—there are no right or wrong answers; there are only answers that are true for you. They are as unique as you are.

You will be asked the same question several times, as each time you will come up with a new, but equally important, answer. You are the only one who really knows your worthiness, so let it all out. You will see how many things you are worthy of—it is amazing. Please jot all your answers below the question—if you would like to add more things, take an additional piece of paper and let it flow.

What are you worthy of? *I'm worthy of...* _____

_____

What are you worthy of? *I'm worthy of...* _____

_____

What are you worthy of? *I'm worthy of...* _____

_____

What are you worthy of? *I'm worthy of...* _____

_____

What are you worthy of? *I'm worthy of...* _____

_____

What are you worthy of? *I'm worthy of...* _____

_____

What are you worthy of? *I'm worthy of...* _____

_____

What are you worthy of? *I'm worthy of...* _____

_____

What are you worthy of? *I'm worthy of...* _____

_____

Have you filled in all the spaces? Great! Have you maybe even added some more answers? Wonderful! Or maybe have you just written three things down and said, "I'm done, that's all"? That is also absolutely all right. It might be the first time you are consciously listening to your inner voice. It might be also the first time that you are pursuing your own self-worth. It is great that you have entered this path of self-discovery and self-realization, as it is a perfect way to give a solid foundation to a fulfilling life. It makes such a difference when you look people in the eye and see a spark there—you see their spirit then and you know they live with purpose and their life has meaning. Nobody can bestow it upon you—you need to find it within you. And now you have undertaken some steps leading to enhancing a very sound self-worth.

There is so much that you are worthy of—much more than you have listed above. I have been leading many people through this process and have seen that almost everyone stops after 2-3 minutes saying, "That's it! I'm done"—that's exactly when the biggest adventure begins: we start the greatest exploration at the point where your rational mind thinks you have said all that was there to say. You are worthy of so many things! Your inner voice tells you the same—you KNOW that. But you have learned to ignore that voice, that feeling of what's right, and instead you have learned to listen to others. It's now that you are about to begin a hidden treasure journey. Enjoy!

You will search inside again and give voice to your truth; you will look for your hidden treasures—and there are plenty of them.

Take a big breath. And another deep breath. Leave the world where it is: Out there. Now, it's about you. Just about you. Take another big breath. Breathe in. Breathe out. Yawn. Sigh. . .

Great! Now you are ready to begin with the Step 2.

STEP 2 – Your Physical Wisdom

Most of us have had the experience that various thoughts and emotions are reflected in different parts of our body. When we get stressed, our stomach often reacts with contractions. When we get angry, our hands tend to clench into a fist. When we fall in love, our heart starts beating faster at the sight of the beloved person. When we have a new, fascinating idea, we forget the rest of the body, its need to eat, drink, or sleep, dwelling temporarily just in our head, bringing our idea to life. Our back starts hurting when we carry too much psychical load on our shoulders. We sometimes get an intuitive "gut feeling". We happen to feel a big lump in the throat when we are at a loss of words or not able to express ourselves, etc. There are many more examples showing how external information influences our body. On the other hand, our body often knows quite precisely what we would need to undertake to achieve a state of well-being. The question is, *"Are we listening?"*

Our body experiences and registers feelings and emotions; it stores information and is endowed with "physical wisdom". The next sequence of questions is to see what our body wisdom tells us. Let's begin.

Heart

Put your hand on your heart. Breathe deeply. Relax. Feel the beat of your heart and its energy. Ask your heart: *"What am I worthy of?"*

Listen to the answer from within, say out loud whatever you have heard and write it down:

My heart says I'm worthy of ... _____

_____

My heart says I'm worthy of ... _____

_____

My heart says I'm worthy of ... _____

_____

My heart says I'm worthy of ... _____

_____

Stomach

Most of us undergo much stress in the everyday life. Very often our stomach suffers from the pressure we are exposed to: it clenches, which results in a stomach ache affecting our eating and digestion. So let's explore this sensitive area.

Put both hands over your stomach area, just below your diaphragm. Now ask this stress-prone part of your body: *"What am I worthy of?"*

Listen to the answer from within; it is ok if it takes time to emerge. Repeat loud what you have heard and write it down:

The area around of my stomach says I'm worthy of ... _____

_____

The area around of my stomach says I'm worthy of ... _____

_____

The area around of my stomach says I'm worthy of ... _____

_____

The area around of my stomach says I'm worthy of ... _____

_____

The area around of my stomach says I'm worthy of ... _____

_____

Head

Now touch your head—it's where thoughts get processed, facts put together, your perception sorted out. It is the center of your logical thinking. You can massage your head bringing focus to the part of your body busy all the time processing information, learning new things, creating new neuronal pathways, sending signals out to the body, etc. New ideas constantly emerge, are categorized and evaluated. It's a very busy part of your body.

Ask your head: *"What am I worthy of?"* and listen to the manifold replies you will receive. Say out loud whatever you have heard and write it down:

My head says I'm worthy of ... _____

_____

My head says I'm worthy of ... _____

_____

My head says I'm worthy of ... _____

_____

My head says I'm worthy of ... _____

_____

My head says I'm worthy of ... _____

_____

Tummy

You sometimes get that "gut feeling". It is not rational; nevertheless, you know that it is good to follow this inner voice. So now put your hand on your tummy in the area of your navel—we have so many feelings there—what does your gut feeling say, *"What are you worthy of?"*

Listen attentively to the answer from within, say out loud whatever you have heard and write it down:

My gut feeling says I'm worthy of ... _____

_____

My gut feeling says I'm worthy of ... _____

_____

My gut feeling says I'm worthy of ... _____

_____

My gut feeling says I'm worthy of ... _____

_____

My gut feeling says I'm worthy of ... _____

_____

My gut feeling says I'm worthy of ... _____

_____

Throat

Put your hand on your throat now; massage it gently. It is such an important place—it's where your thoughts and ideas become reality. Your thoughts become words, your feelings get expressed, and your inner life becomes externalized to the outside world.

I am sure you can recall situations when you felt speechless, not being able to produce the right statement. You were short of words or did not know how to express yourself. This can lead to a feeling of suffocating or having a big lump in your throat. Alternatively, you might have experienced a situation when your mouth couldn't shut because of a tirade, which you regretted later. What does your throat say: *"What are you worthy of?"*

My throat says that I'm worthy of ... _____

_____

My throat says that I'm worthy of ... _____

_____

My throat says that I'm worthy of ... _____

_____

My throat says that I'm worthy of ... _____

_____

Great job! You have been listening to and voicing your physical wisdom; you have let your body speak and reveal what it knows that you are worthy of.

You might have left some spaces empty—that's absolutely all right; you will notice that your focus of attention has been changing and, from now on, you will start thinking of your worthiness more and more.

Please return later to the points you have not completed, asking yourself the Question. You may suddenly get the answers while preoccupied with something else. Jot down your realization the first possible moment, adding it to the great list you have started recording today.

STEP 3 – Specific Areas of Your Life

Now let's have a look at different areas of life and how your sense of worth corresponds with them. We will have a look at some specific areas of your activity where you will be able to formulate what you feel you are worthy of in each.

What are you worthy of in the area of family life?

In the area of my family life, I am worthy of ... _____

_____

In the area of my family life, I am worthy of ... _____

_____

In the area of my family life, I am worthy of ... _____

_____

In the area of my family life, I am worthy of ... _____

_____

In the area of my family life, I am worthy of ... _____

_____

In the area of my family life, I am worthy of ... _____

_____

In the area of my family life, I am worthy of ... _____

_____

In the area of my family life, I am worthy of ... _____

_____

In the area of my family life, I am worthy of ... _____

_____

HOW WOULD YOUR FAMILY LIFE BE DIFFERENT
IF YOU WERE TO OPERATE FROM THE PARADIGM
OF WORTHINESS?

What are you worthy of in the area of love?

In the area of love, I am worthy of ... _____

_____

In the area of love, I am worthy of ... _____

_____

In the area of love, I am worthy of ... _____

_____

In the area of love, I am worthy of ... _____

_____

What are you worthy of in the area of spirituality?

In the area of spirituality, I am worthy of ... _____

_____

In the area of spirituality, I am worthy of ... _____

_____

In the area of spirituality, I am worthy of ... _____

_____

In the area of spirituality, I am worthy of ... _____

_____

HOW WOULD YOUR LIFE BE DIFFERENT IF YOU WERE TO OPERATE FROM THE PARADIGM OF WORTHINESS IN THE AREA OF LOVE?

HOW WOULD YOUR SPIRITUAL LIFE BE DIFFERENT IF YOU WERE TO OPERATE FROM THE PARADIGM OF WORTHINESS?

What are you worthy of in the area of health?

In the area of health, I am worthy of ... _____

_____

In the area of health, I am worthy of ... _____

_____

In the area of health, I am worthy of ... _____

_____

In the area of health, I am worthy of ... _____

_____

What are you worthy of in the area of relationships?

In the area of relationships, I am worthy of ... _____

_____

In the area of relationships, I am worthy of ... _____

_____

In the area of relationships, I am worthy of ... _____

_____

In the area of relationships, I am worthy of ... _____

_____

HOW WOULD YOUR HEALTH BE DIFFERENT
IF YOU WERE TO OPERATE FROM THE PARADIGM
OF WORTHINESS?

HOW WOULD YOUR RELATIONSHIPS BE DIFFERENT
IF YOU WERE TO OPERATE FROM THE PARADIGM
OF WORTHINESS?

What are you worthy of in the area of creativity?

In the area of creativity, I am worthy of ... _____

_____

In the area of creativity, I am worthy of ... _____

_____

In the area of creativity, I am worthy of ... _____

_____

In the area of creativity, I am worthy of ... _____

_____

What are you worthy of in the area of education?

In the area of education, I am worthy of ... _____

_____

In the area of education, I am worthy of ... _____

_____

In the area of education, I am worthy of ... _____

_____

In the area of education, I am worthy of ... _____

_____

HOW WOULD YOUR CREATIVITY BE DIFFERENT
IF YOU WERE TO OPERATE FROM THE PARADIGM
OF WORTHINESS?

HOW WOULD YOUR EDUCATION BE DIFFERENT
IF YOU WERE TO OPERATE FROM THE PARADIGM
OF WORTHINESS?

What are you worthy of in the area of work & career?

In the area of work and career, I am worthy of... _____

_____

In the area of work and career, I am worthy of... _____

_____

In the area of work and career, I am worthy of... _____

_____

In the area of work and career, I am worthy of... _____

_____

What are you worthy of in the area of money?

In the area of money, I am worthy of... _____

_____

In the area of money, I am worthy of... _____

_____

In the area of money, I am worthy of... _____

_____

In the area of money, I am worthy of... _____

_____

HOW WOULD YOUR WORK AND CAREER BE DIFFERENT IF YOU WERE TO OPERATE FROM THE PARADIGM OF WORTHINESS?

HOW WOULD YOUR FINANCIAL SITUATION BE DIFFERENT IF YOU WERE TO OPERATE FROM THE PARADIGM OF WORTHINESS?

What are you worthy of in the area of your social life?

In the area of my social life, I am worthy of... _____

_____

In the area of my social life, I am worthy of... _____

_____

In the area of my social life, I am worthy of... _____

_____

In the area of my social life, I am worthy of... _____

_____

What are you worthy of in the area of fun and joy?

In the area of fun and joy, I am worthy of... _____

_____

In the area of fun and joy, I am worthy of... _____

_____

In the area of fun and joy, I am worthy of... _____

_____

In the area of fun and joy, I am worthy of... _____

_____

How would your social life be different if you were to operate from the paradigm of worthiness?

How would your life be different if you were to operate from the paradigm of worthiness in the area of fun and joy?

What are you worthy of in the area travel and adventure?

In the area of travel and adventure, I am worthy of ... _____

_____

In the area of travel and adventure, I am worthy of ... _____

_____

In the area of travel and adventure, I am worthy of ... _____

_____

In the area of travel and adventure, I am worthy of ... _____

_____

What are you worthy of regarding food & eating habits?

In the area of food and eating habits, I am worthy of ... _____

_____

In the area of food and eating habits, I am worthy of ... _____

_____

In the area of food and eating habits, I am worthy of ... _____

_____

In the area of food and eating habits, I am worthy of ... _____

_____

HOW WOULD YOUR LIFE BE DIFFERENT IF YOU WERE TO OPERATE FROM THE PARADIGM OF WORTHINESS AS FAR AS TRAVELING AND ADVENTURES ARE CONCERNED?

HOW WOULD YOUR FOOD AND EATING HABITS BE DIFFERENT IF YOU WERE TO OPERATE FROM THE PARADIGM OF WORTHINESS?

What are you worthy of as far as beauty in your life is concerned?

As far as beauty in my life is concerned, I am worthy of ... _____

_____

As far as beauty in my life is concerned, I am worthy of ... _____

_____

As far as beauty in my life is concerned, I am worthy of ... _____

_____

As far as beauty in my life is concerned, I am worthy of ... _____

_____

What are you worthy of in the area of your lifestyle?

In the area of my lifestyle, I am worthy of ... _____

_____

In the area of my lifestyle, I am worthy of ... _____

_____

In the area of my lifestyle, I am worthy of ... _____

_____

In the area of my lifestyle, I am worthy of ... _____

_____

HOW WOULD YOUR LIFE BE DIFFERENT IF YOU WERE TO OPERATE FROM THE PARADIGM OF WORTHINESS IN THE AREA OF BEAUTY?

HOW WOULD YOUR LIFE STYLE BE DIFFERENT IF YOU WERE TO OPERATE FROM THE PARADIGM OF WORTHINESS?

Congratulations! You've done excellent work. How do you feel now? Every single answer you have spoken out and written down is like a precious gem that you have searched for and found within yourself. Together they will constitute a foundation of your solid self-esteem, so the more you find, the stronger the foundation you are creating.

Take time to explore the areas that you couldn't relate to at first, where you wrote just one or two answers and could not think of anything else. Explore the topic looking for more—let's compare it to returning to a goldmine to look around for some nuggets you overlooked before. All answers, which seem invisible now, are your personal wealth, your inner richness. You are in a possession of a goldmine and you may decide to just own it, merely entertaining a thought of some nuggets still left inside, but enjoying no benefits of the hidden treasure. Or you can choose to make some effort, go deeper inside and bring them out to the daylight where you can consciously use them.

You may also feel that there are some more areas you would like to explore. Please do—you are a unique individual and you alone know all your worth. So listen to your inner voice telling you what you are worthy of, no matter what your surrounding environment is trying to convey to you. You will see how much your life is going to change because slowly you will not accept anything that does not correspond with your worthiness any more.

You will notice an astonishing change: the moment you become clear about your worthiness and claim it for yourself, the world around you will accept it too. Your environment reacts to the way you are, which is based on your self-worth. Automatically, your awareness of what you are worthy of, resulting from having done some inner work, will make you feel more fulfilled and satisfied with your life.

CHAPTER 5

SENSE OF COMPETENCE:

I CAN DO IT!

Along with the feeling of self-worth, a sense of competence is the second element of your self-esteem. By answering the questions you were preparing a very solid foundation. Now it can be used to lay the ground floor of competence upon it, creating the basis for a beautiful and solid house of healthy self-esteem. Your mind and spirit can function better within a stable construction.

You are worthy of expressing your authentic self. You design and build the house yourself. Remember, your creation can be influenced by others only as much as you allow; if you think they are influencing or dominating your design, make the borders clear and maybe even put some fence around your place. Its purpose is not to keep others away but to remind you about your right to owning your life and your decisions. You may let those who are supportive and whom you love in, but you have a full right to keep those who pull you down at bay. You are worthy of healthy relationships. Every fence can be climbed over by a pushy person, so you need to remember that it is your right to ask every intruder to leave your space. You are worthy of having as much space around you as you need.

You are also worthy of growth; so let's enhance your sense of competence, focusing on all your achievements, successes and all the things you have learned up to now.

What are your strengths? What are your core abilities? What have you learned and achieved in your life? Do you often acknowledge your successes? Were your achievements and victory moments celebrated when you were a child? Or were you brought up in a culture of enforced humbleness where there was lots of criticism and little praise?

As Nathaniel Brandon said, "Of all the judgments we pass in life, none is more important than the judgment we pass on ourselves". So create now the best image of your competence that you can. It will be true and accurate as it is based on the facts from your life.

You will now emphasize aspects you have never acknowledged consciously before or have not regarded worth mentioning.

Please list 5 words that describe the best in you:

Example: *joyful, radiant, empathic, determined, etc.*

1. _____

2. _____

3. _____

4. _____

5. _____

Please list 5 of your strengths:

Example: *I'm very patient. I'm an excellent cook.*

1. _____

2. _____

3. _____

4. _____

5. _____

Please list 5 of your core abilities:

Example: *I'm very exact in my job as a bookkeeper.*
I can bring peace into any conflict in my family.

1. _____

2. _____

3. _____

4. _____

5. _____

Please list 5 achievements of which you are most proud. You do not need to list heroic deeds here, just think of actions that you needed to accomplish in order to step out of your comfort zone—and that required real courage. The first step away from the old routine often requires you to be really brave and can be counted as a huge success.

Example: *I travelled abroad by myself.*
I got braces at the age of 37 though I felt too old for that.

1. _____

2. _____

3. _____

4. _____

5. _____

Please list all your achievements—as many as you can but at least 1 per completed year of your life (if you are 52 for instance—list at least 52 achievements, if you are 26—at least 26, though preferably more, and so on).

Include even the tiniest accomplishment and learned skill—list them all below. Don't evaluate them or compare; each was equally important.

Example: *I have learned to speak my mother tongue.* (Sounds funny? Yes, I know, but since learning a language is one of the most complex challenges for the brain—learning to speak a language, be it your mother tongue or a foreign language, is a success!)
I have learned to eat with knife and fork.
I have graduated form the primary school.

1. _____

2. _____

3. _____

4. _____

5. _____

6. _____

7. _____

8. _____

9. _____

10. _____

11. _____

12. _____

13. _____

14. _____

15. _____

16. _____

17. _____

18. _____

19. _____

20. _____

21. _____

22. _____

23. _____

24. _____

25. _____

26. _____

27. _____

28. _____

29. _____

30. _____

31. _____

32. _____

33. _____

34. _____

35. _____

36. _____

37. _____

38. _____

39. _____

40. _____

41. _____

42. _____

43. _____

44. _____

45. _____

46. _____

47. _____

48. _____

49. _____

50. _____

51. _____

52. _____

53. _____

54. _____

55. _____

56. _____

57. _____

58. _____

59. _____

60. _____

61. _____

62. _____

63. _____

64. _____

65. _____

66. _____

67. _____

68. _____

69. _____

70. _____

71. _____

72. _____

73. _____

74. _____

75. _____

76. _____

77. _____

78. _____

79. _____

80. _____

81. _____

82. _____

83. _____

84. _____

85. _____

86. _____

87. _____

88. _____

89. _____

90. _____

91. _____

92. _____

93. _____

94. _____

95. _____

96. _____

97. _____

98. _____

99. _____

100. _____

If you are 101 or older, you can stop here knowing you are absolutely awesome and one of your greatest life achievements is to have recognized that it is never too late to introduce changes enhancing your life-quality and the way you feel about yourself.

If you are younger and have filled in one success per year of your life, you have done an excellent job—great! You may want to go back again and again and add more and more achievements. You must already feel how fulfilling it is to see a list of one's own achievements giving you a sense of competence and seeing that there is still so much more in your life worth mentioning. Even if you cannot think of anything at the moment, it does not matter. You are not used to thinking in superlatives about yourself—you need time to allow yourself to acknowledge the greatness in you. And you do not do it just for yourself; acknowledging yourself, you allow your family, friends, teammates, colleagues, etc. to relate to you differently and also inspire them to look at their own strengths. As

Marianne Williamson states: "As we let our own light shine, we consciously give other people permission to do the same." You are worthy of letting your qualities shine. Just stay appreciative about what you have already listed—no matter if there were just a few achievements or quite a number—stay assured that if you cherish all that you have accomplished, other positive memories will surface as well.

If, however, you have not written anything in, don't worry—you can start changing your old habits now. Simply grab something to write with and go back to the beginning of this chapter and jot down all your strengths, abilities, achievements, etc. You will see what a great feeling it is to see the list of your successes. You will feel how much it enhances your sense of competence because you know that these are facts and all these accomplishments have really taken place in your life.

Congratulations!

CHAPTER 6

LIGHT AND SHADOW:

EMBRACE YOUR WHOLENESS

You have laid the foundation of self-worth and put the ground floor of competence on top of it. Now you are ready to re-construct your house successfully into a healthy self-esteem building based on this solid foundation.

As you were growing up, you were building your house to the best of your knowledge and capacities. You might have enjoyed a supportive environment and it became a good-looking and comfortable home for your mind and spirit to live in. Maybe, however, you constructed it in tough circumstances, with scarcity of good building material, and under the influence of others' opinions and decisions. You might have sensed dissatisfaction with the results when those influences were no longer present, but you didn't feel worthy or competent enough to reconstruct your own building according to your own vision. As the result, your mind and spirit would rather "keep wandering around" instead of "moving in" and you might have experienced the following: a feeling of inner emptiness, senselessness of life, powerlessness, apathy or maybe even obsessions or addictions to escape the reality and self-judgmental thoughts. That was then. Now, after all the processes you have undergone, you have the means to take a stand for yourself, ready to take responsibility for your life.

Remember, you are rebuilding and redesigning your house on your own. You are the architect and you are the builder. No one else has the power to decide what it is going to look like and how strong the construction is going to be—it is up to you now: you decide how important it is for you and how much effort you are going to put into it.

Even if there are some old events and past hurts haunting you which can be compared to some old trash on your lawn, unappealing colors on the walls or furniture that does not match your sense of style and beauty, you can choose to either complain about it, feeling a victim of the circumstances, or clear the space, redesign the interior, and plant beautiful flowers in your garden instead.

Trash will not stop stinking by your talking about how unpleasant it is or just holding your nose; you need to make a conscious decision to get rid of it. You need to decide to take the action of letting it go, leaving the old hurts and events behind where they belong: in the past. When you look at them again and again, you only make yourself suffer. I am not questioning the seriousness of what had happened, I am just trying to make it clear that by digging through this old trash, the person who is punished and hurts continually is you, because not only it did happen to you back then, but also you keep activating the thoughts and feelings about these past events in the present, so now you have both the hurting memory and the warmed-up negative feelings you are repeatedly activating within your system.

The old events and hurts have caused some shadows in you to arise. What are the so-called shadows? These are thoughts, negative feelings, fears, self-limiting beliefs, blockages, self-sabotaging habits, wounds and behaviors which arose as your reaction to misuse, be it verbal, physical, etc. They are your response to some misbehavior towards you stripping you of your dignity and your feeling of worth. Marshall B. Rosenberg suggests *"We only feel dehumanized when we get trapped in the derogatory images of other people or thoughts of wrongness about ourselves"*[2]. The good news is that no one ever has managed to take your worth away, though they might have succeeded in making you believe you are not worthy. Your self-worth has always been there, although it might have been suppressed into a state of hibernation, waiting for spring to return and bring conditions for your worthiness to blossom and flourish again. And this moment is right now.

Aware of your dark sides, which can be compared to some dark corners in your beautifully redesigned house, you might tend to ignore them or even consciously make them unnoticeable, drawing curtains tight together, ashamed of what could be found there. You do not let anyone into these rooms, often locking them up, throwing the key away, and pretending there is nothing behind those doors. However, as Mark Twain said, "The worst loneliness is not to be comfortable with yourself".

Opening these doors one by one, casting the light upon what's inside, and consciously clearing the space of the old clutter is the only way to embrace and heal your connection with the suppressed areas. To live pretending that they do not exist causes inner tension. Not expressed directly, it colors your self-expression preventing you from being your authentic self. You may sometimes have a feeling that you do not come across the way you would like to or you wonder why people do not see you the way you are—it might be that your inner tension unconsciously influences the way you communicate as well as your emotions and robs you of your inner peace.

Imagine you have got a thorn in your foot—would you be able to walk joyfully, dance passionately and run with all your might? Of course not, not as long as the thorn is stuck in your flesh. On one hand you'd be hindered in your self-expression; on the other, the constant pain would make you impatient, irritated, and discontent. It works the same way with shadows. Their existence in your system causes inner tension influencing your overall well-being. Only a true change in your attitude towards your shadows, expressed by readiness to look into them, will lead to more balance, self-acceptance, inner peace and improved self-esteem. So it might not be enough to say, "I'm worthy of peace and happiness"—go one step backwards instead and declare, "I'm worthy of creating a solid basis for my self-esteem".

You need to open the windows, let the fresh air in and cast the light onto the dark corners. Only by acknowledging the existence of your shadows and embracing them, will you be ready to start working with them consciously and become complete as a human being. Some of the clutter might even turn out to be treasure, which you were unable to notice due to the dust and dirt layers disguising it. However, you will be able to use it as a treasure once you have stopped referring to it as a disturbing burden only. When you let go of the attachment to a particular shadow, for instance an old act of injustice done to you, you will be free to see the incident as such and either disconnect yourself from it emotionally or recognize what insights and strength it gave you.

Some shadows may stay as your trait forever, which is not a problem, and once you are aware, you will consciously ride this energy, instead of letting it pull you behind in an uncontrollable manner. For example, if you have a tendency to become defensive and argue with people when you sense injustice, you might want to apply it to a bigger cause and instead of complaining and quarreling with your neighbor or co-workers, you might choose to make street children your cause and with all your might fight successfully for their education and rights— feeling the injustice in their fate will make your efforts very effective. But if you do not acknowledge the fact that a feeling of injustice triggers strong feelings in you, you will continue reacting to the events in your life, failing to notice the driving force underneath it.

Figuratively speaking, as long as you have a body, you will have shadows. Even if you turn your face towards the light, you will not stop being endowed with a shadow. Only when you have become a spirit, will you cast no shadow. But you are still in your body, alive, trying to make the best out of your life. So the point is not to try to get rid of all your shadows, but rather to face them by acknowledging and embracing your imperfections, and checking all the dark corners in respect to what really had collected there. You might even find some treasures there. You will for sure gain mental and emotional freedom, which will allow you to get rid of those that act as an unnecessary burden to your everyday life.

As humans we will always be imperfect in some respect – and that's what makes us perfect humans. Once we have accepted our "dark side", our old wounds, triggers, weaknesses, shortcomings, and imperfections, which we try to hide although all other humans have them as well—we will feel relief and freedom. When you admit you have got a weakness, you never need to fear that someone might find it out, as it is not a secret any more. As Wayne W. Dyer says, "Accept that you are enough. You don't need to be anything that you are not"[3]. Our shadows are nothing to deny or be afraid of. Although they are marked with hurt, pain and are often experienced as a blockage, when released and worked with, they turn into our friends and show us our light within. Debbie Ford, one of the most prominent shadow workers states that "The Shadow Process gives us access to loving all of ourselves. This deep and profound work teaches us how to love each and every aspect of our humanity." And you are worthy of self-love, self-care, self-respect and self-appreciation.

The essential question is: Where is your focus in your life, on light or on shadow? Do you perceive beauty and synchronicity in things or do you mainly complain about what doesn't work? Do you have a feeling that the universe is plotting to do you good or are you expecting to fail again? Do you make your past into a part of your present moment by carrying the old events along, referring to them as fresh and making them the theme of your life?

Don't you often carry your past around still today, making it a part of your present moment? May it become what it is, i.e. the past. Having dealt with your shadows, you gain the freedom to see them for what they are: the results of some past events. Yes, you are worthy of freedom from the past; you are worthy of staying in the joyful creation of the present and in a hopeful expectation of what is to come. I have witnessed people walk a long way from dwelling in past hurts and pains to the joyful lightness of being in the present moment, so I know it is possible for you too. "Pain results from a judgment you have made about a situation. Remove the judgment and the pain disappears. Judgment is based on a previous experience. Your idea about a thing or situation is created from a prior idea about that thing—which is based on a prior idea, which again, is based on a prior idea. Each negative thought or judgment sits on another like building blocks," Lauri DeJulian, an amazing shadow worker who helped me transform my life, would tell me.

Probably, as many others, you too have practiced for years listening to others' beliefs and convictions of who you are and what you should become, perfecting that input along the way to such an extent, that you have forgotten what you know for yourself as true. Jack Canfield makes us aware of the fact that "All too often we're filled with negative and limiting beliefs. We're filled with doubt. We're filled with guilt or with a sense of unworthiness. We have a lot of assumptions about the way the world is that are actually wrong". If your shadows are really strong, pull you down and prevent you from rebuilding your "house" of self-esteem the way you would like it to become, in order to start living the life you have always wanted to lead, you might think of contacting a specialist in this field, such as a good and experienced shadow-worker, an Emotional Freedom Technique (EFT) practitioner, a psychologist or a psychotherapist specialized in a shadow-work, a skilled hypnotherapist etc. It is also transformational to learn how to consciously reconnect with your Spirit, so that the shadows can weaken and slowly lose their grip on you due to the power of your inner light and the increased vibration of your thoughts and feelings. Sonia Choquette, a worldwide respected vibrational healer and an extraordinary six-sensory teacher, whom I regard myself lucky to have studied with because that enabled me to undergo my personal transformation, which raised the level of functioning, says "As you continue to strengthen your relationship with your Spirit, the mental chatter of your ego will quiet down. The suspicions, insecurities, second-guessing, defensive dialogues, and ruminating over your less-than-successful past will begin to decrease. And with this newfound quiet, your attention will be drawn to the sound, feeling, and vibration of your inner voice. You'll begin to hear your guidance . . . your inner radar will kick in and start to direct you toward your deepest goals."[4]

Life does not have to be mainly struggle and suffering as many people experience it. It can be filled with lightness and joy. Don't you feel worthy of a fun-filled happy existence? If a doubt "Do I deserve it?" or "Would that be proper?" etc., creeps out as your first reaction, please analyze it. You will realize that it is some past conditioning, directing you to such limited thinking. Give yourself permission to break free. It might seem hard at the beginning, especially when your surroundings neither understand, nor support, nor approve of the changes you are striving for. If that's the case, you may need to step out and find a new community, which shares your aspirations. Human beings have a need of belonging; people will sometimes sacrifice their growth to avoid being ostracized. Be assured that there are "your peeps" out there—you just need to find them. You are never alone in your striving for personal development.

CHAPTER 7

❧ · ❧

FORGIVENESS AND
SELF-FORGIVENESS

Forgiveness is like growing a flower in your garden. It doesn't happen by itself. First of all, you need to want to grow a flower at all; likewise you put an intention forward that you are ready to let forgiveness enter your life. Then you create space where your flower can be planted by removing wild growing weeds. Likewise, you get ready to let go of old beliefs of right and wrong and you are ready to step back from the feeling of righteousness. Once the seed has been planted, you need to tend to it; it's not enough to just have an intention but it involves some active approach. You water the seed and hope it will sprout. Likewise, you water the seed of forgiveness with prayers or wishes to heal and let old grudges and judgments go. Actually, what you need to let go the most is clinging to the righteousness of your judgments. What makes you withhold your forgiveness from yourself and others is your feeling of what's right and wrong. You established a certain code of validation and judged people and situations accordingly. To forgive now means releasing others and yourself from the rigid construct of old beliefs, which became your reference point that you based your judgments upon. They became a cage of suffering that you trapped yourself in. Don't hold it against yourself now—you have built up your world in a certain way, to the best of your abilities, stemming from your past experiences, in order to protect and serve your survival. You have an opportunity to reconstruct your world now according to your conscious decisions of how you want to thrive. How can you do that?

You start at the level of your own suffering. Stop judging what happened; just feel the burden of it. How long do you still want to carry it around? Feel the rigid cage of "should" and "shouldn't" causing your judgments, which keep you away from a direct experience of happiness and love. When you feel "he shouldn't have done it" or "I should have been treated in a better way" etc., you create an illusory blueprint that you start using as a reference point for your feelings and emotions.

Wouldn't you rather give it away in order to live free of the old pain? To forgive does not mean to forget. To forgive means to let the old wounds heal. It does not mean to diminish the other person's wrongdoing. It means to allow your self to live without the venom of resentment and mourning. When you let the forgiveness unfold like a petals of a flower bud, you will discover so much more beauty in your life. You will be able to enjoy anew, have a fresh look at things, and base your decisions not on what you resist and keep running away from, but you become finally free to choose what you truly want. When you forgive, you give yourself the best gift ever. It can be compared to life without taking daily baths in the venom of old negative emotions. Applying forgiveness in your life is an expression of self-care. Could you consider letting the old pain go just out of love and respect for yourself? Ask yourself, "Am I worthy of happiness? Am I worthy of freedom of old pain? Am I worthy of living without guilt? Am I worthy of leading a fulfilled life? Am I worthy of allowing forgiveness into my life? Am I worthy of loving my self and acting upon it? Am I worthy of attaining inner peace?"

It hurts when you look at the event again, so you might subconsciously tend to suppress the memory. Why does it hurt so much? Because you felt disrespected, invalidated, violated in your humanity; you felt someone stripped you off your dignity; you began feeling worthless in some respect. And the inner conflict started because the core of you, your higher self knows, that you are always worthy and nothing can rob you of it. You felt it but you stopped seeing it. Then you turned around and asked the world to confirm your worthiness.

People choose different ways of dealing with it: you may, for example, have fallen into the trap of victimhood, expecting the world to validate you by acknowledging the wrongness of what happened. So you would talk about the past, opening the wound again and again, not letting it heal out. You might have chosen to keep stiff upper lip, unattached to feelings, and pretended nothing had happened; in this way trying to get the confirmation from outside that even though you feel damaged goods inside, the world still sees you as a whole and complete. However, you cannot expect other hurt beings—as almost everyone is carrying some pain in them—to heal you. You need to allow the healing from within. And the healing is called forgiveness. Incorporating forgiveness into your life will help you feel worthy again.

It is crucial, however, to remember that you do not validate the other person's actions by forgiving them—this is the most common reason why people do not to allow forgiveness. Stay assured that the other person witnessed his or her own wrongdoing. They were there, and they perceived what was happening. They might have suppressed the memory due to the feeling of guilt or misinterpreted the facts to be able to cope with them, but the perception of the situation got stored in their sub-consciousness. They might have even already realized and regretted what happened, but their ego was too strong to come and apologize, like yours was too strong to allow you to forgive. They might have even wanted to apologize but your resistance against them kept them at bay. The moment you truly forgive someone and let go of the expectations that they should have made up for or, at least, acknowledged what you perceive as their wrongdoing, some resistance dam on the energy level crumbles down. It sometimes happens that the person you kept at bay by your resentments suddenly turns up and expresses their apology or even love. For this to happen, you need to create the space of forgiveness first. Even if the person doesn't come up in person, so called "negative karmic bonds" get dissolved by your act of forgiveness, as you release them from all the blame that you assigned them.

Your shadows casting darkness over some aspects of your self-worth came into being through what you perceived in the past as hurts, violence, injustice, and abuse. You wish those who acted in this way should realize their wrongdoing and feel sorry for what they have done to you. You judge their past behavior as negative and, automatically, you move yourself into a victim position, which you leave first after they have apologized to you; consequently, you make your forgiveness fully dependent on others.

Forgiving someone means projecting a multiple expectation and judgment onto them:

1. They should have it done differently
2. They should admit their wrongdoing and be sorry now
3. They should come to apologize

And, in many cases, only then you are ready to consider forgiving them.

In this way, your inner freedom, lightness, and happiness resulting from letting go of old hurts fully depend on others and their choice to act according to your expectations or not. Do you realize how much power you give away in this way?

What about approaching it in a different way: forgive not others, but yourself. It might be a new concept to you but keep exploring it further as it might result in a big release. When you forgive yourself, you free yourself from your expectations towards others, which might keep you stuck in the old hurts. It is a switch from the way of thinking, "They did something to me", to "Actually, it was I who allowed whatever they did to hurt me". I am not trying to diminish the hurt that occurred. If you had been abused, it caused a wound that now may result in you feeling disempowered, abused, helpless or worthless. Physical or emotional pain is, of course, a pain and it cannot be denied. However, an interesting phenomenon occurs there: if you think it wasn't done to you on purpose, you tend to forget the event easily. You don't even need to forgive and the event is erased from your memory. If you, however, think that someone did something intentionally, you start judging how bad they are and grow an attachment towards the negative interpretation of the event, allowing an attitude "How could they have done that to me?" It etches in your consciousness as injustice, hurt, or abuse and you either start fighting with the memory of the event or you develop resistance in this field. You believe that staying resentful and holding a grudge against somebody, will punish them for what they have done. But it's you and you alone who gets punished by re-living the old situation anew. You create your own hell: you send yourself into the same suffering again and again. Just by experiencing the pain perpetually, you won't make them understand what they have done to you. It's you who suffers from lack of letting go, no one else. Do you really want to go on suffering? You are worthy of happiness, which is not possible while you are holding yourself in your own hell. You have ended up there because you haven't known better; so don't get angry with yourself for that. You don't need to feel helpless—there is a way out of suffering. It is called self-forgiveness.

It is you, and you only, who choose the way you treat the past events. You can try out a new approach now: please think of an event that you have felt resentful about till today and describe this specific situation with a purely mechanical approach: This and that happened there and then.

Let me tell you a story of a man, Tim, who as a child was regularly beaten up by his father, which led to his deep feeling of uncertainty and unworthiness. When he told me the story, it sounded very dramatic, much pain, disappointment, and self-loathing involved. Tim felt a victim of a cruel angry father who would destroy him instead of nourishing him, his only child, giving him love and support. He took his father's behavior as a benchmark of his own worth and started living accordingly. He would feel unloved, disrespected, his needs of closeness unmet. His life mirrored it back to him because it was all he expected to get, being convinced he was unworthy of anything better. He also developed self-loathing for his own body and would not respect its needs, putting too much strain on the body at work and neglecting its needs of good nourishment and movement.

Then Tim tried the new approach. He started a process of forgiving himself. His new record of the past would read: "My father was beating me up till I would lose my consciousness. That made me believe I was unlovable, unwanted, and unworthy. I learnt that my body wasn't worth taking care of and applied this pattern all life long. Now I can see that my father was unable to share love because he was raised by parents that withdrew from their feelings. He was not able to cope with challenges of his life, so he channeled his frustration onto his family. His acts of violence had nothing to do with me. I was around and he used me as an object to let his anger out, but I was not a direct cause of his attacks. I release him from the blame I assigned him. And I forgive myself now, for having thought all these years long that I was a bad child deserving bad treatment. I forgive myself now, for having expected love from a man who never felt it come from his parents. I forgive myself for continuing to misuse and disrespect my body, like he did it. I forgive myself for having lived following the old patterns for so many years. I promise myself to love myself and extend my love to others. I allow myself to feel good about myself. I am worthy of happiness and love."

Self-forgiveness starts when you take a look at the past events from a different angle. You begin to see that it may have been attributed to your perception, expectation, inability, ignorance, immaturity to cope with things, lack of experience in a certain field, attachment, or judgment of people and situations that made you suffer.

If you can see that you were responsible for a past event to have become painful to you, the only person that needs forgiveness is you, not anyone else. You forgive yourself for not having known better in all those situations, which frees a lot of energy, and helps you move on with life.

If you plant a flower of forgiveness in your soul, it will beautify the garden of your life forever. Here is a poem that I wrote in the forgiveness process and used as a daily prayer.

I Forgive Myself

I forgive myself
For having made all the mistakes
Had I known better, I would have chosen differently
So I forgive myself

I forgive myself
For having felt hurt when I didn't feel loved and wanted
They never promised me they would, so it was just my unmet
expectation
So I forgive myself

I forgive myself
For believing them when they said I'm unworthy
They didn't see my light and spoke out of their shadows
So I forgive myself

I forgive myself
For feeling scared and getting hurt when they acted out of anger
I know now it was not about me – it was their inability to cope
with life better
So I forgive myself

I forgive myself
For the suffering when I felt I don't belong
It made me journey inwards and find my spirit, my true home
So I forgive myself

I forgive myself
For feeling let down
They did what they believed was ok – my hurt came from what I
wanted from them
So I forgive myself

I forgive myself
For having believed that my love is worthless
My love is precious – but they were too hurt to open up to it
So I forgive myself

I forgive myself
For having learnt not to love myself
I accepted it was right not to care about myself, but now I know
who I am
So I forgive myself

I forgive myself
For taking things as directed against me
They were just events that took place because the doers were not
happy with their life
So I forgive myself

I forgive myself
For having given my power away, letting them decide for me
I felt fear or didn't know better, but now I'm ready to learn
So I forgive myself
I forgive myself

For having expressed hurtful judgments of myself, which made me judge others too
I've finally tasted the sweetness of love over the bitterness of the critique-poison
So I forgive myself

I forgive myself
For believing I'm unable, I'm small, I don't count
I allow myself to acknowledge the truth that I have gifts and I'm worthy
So I forgive myself

I forgive myself
That it took me so long to learn to forgive
But I was willing to learn
So now I forgive and start to respect myself

CHAPTER 8

WORTHY OF TRUE SUCCESS:

LIVING YOUR HEART'S DESIRE

What is a real success? "Success" is a catchword in today's world. There have been hundreds of books written on different aspects of success, explaining what you need to do to achieve it. However, only a few who had read the books became really successful. Why? You can reach a lot in life when you feel worthy of it. If you don't feel worthy of something, you may wish to achieve it, but you will tend to self-sabotage yourself to stay on the level that your self-worth allows you to achieve in that specific area. Therefore, let's examine the direct connection between your sense of worthiness and success.

What does success mean to you in the first place? Don't look at others' definitions, just feel it in your heart. True success covers all areas of life. Having a leading position in a corporate world but having neither true friends nor good health, is not a real success; it just indicates a competence in a specific area of your life. Take a few moments now to answer these questions.

What does success mean to you? _____

_____

What would an overall success mean to you? _____

_____

Would it mean being loved, happy, feeling safe and secure,

appreciated, having a family? _____

_____

_____

Now consider the following questions and write a summary about what success means to you below. What does living joyfully, having a satisfying job and supportive connections mean? Being able to contribute to others' lives and making a difference? Looking at the end of the day in the mirror rejoicing yet another day of meaningful activities? Enjoying sound health and mobility? Having adventures and traveling the world? Enjoying meaningful conversations with your friends on regular basis and being able to extend your love unconditionally? Having time just for you and being financially carefree? Just jot everything down that comes to your mind, without censoring your thoughts according to the learnt norms.

Success means to me: _____

_____

_____

_____

_____

_____

_____

_____

_____

_____

Don't measure yourself against others and drop all the ego-based concepts of "should" and "deserve". Reach to your heart instead and answer this question. What is your innermost desire that, lived out, would make you feel successful?

_____

_____

_____

_____

When you speak out of your heart, it will resonate with you and give you a sense of fulfillment. It is, however, an approach that many people seek first after the will-powered and mind-driven success has ended in a burnout, heart attack, divorce, or some other disappointing condition. You can use the power of your will for quite a while but, eventually, it is prone to get you feeling worn out, tired, alone, maybe even depressed and done. All actions steered by the will are endowed with the element of "because" and "in order to": I want this job in order to prove to my parents that I can do well on my own. I want to marry a rich person in order to feel really safe and financially secure. I want to have children because it will make my life meaningful. Any belief or reason that contains "because" and "in order to" is conditioned and does not reflect your heart's true desire.

Your will is powered by your ego and tries to fulfill some program which usually becomes a priority and results in ignoring some other vital parts of your personality. As far as the physical level is concerned, it usually ends up with either neglecting your body's needs or exercising it to froth. Neither extreme originates from a state of an inner balance. It might give you some satisfaction of being able to check off yet another item on your "To Do" list, which feeds your ego, but it does not lead to an overall sense of meaning and fulfillment in life, which oftentimes leads to a feeling of emptiness.

Addictions, be it workaholism, alcoholism, eating too much, looking for sex perpetually, watching TV endlessly etc., is a frequent way people deal with this unwelcomed feeling, trying to still it through outer distractions instead of going inwards to align with their true source of happiness, contentment, peace and sense of security.

Your ego is based on the concept of separation, unworthiness, and lack, thus the constant drive to prove, be right, achieve, gain, own, and hoard. Your ego's underlying feeling is fear which induces the following feelings: attachments and clinging, as it fears loss and change; pride, jealousy and envy, as it feels it doesn't have enough and compares oneself to others; as well as desire for more and better, as it never attains the state of being whole and complete, thus always trying to get more and more from outside and tending to fall into anger when not getting what it wants.

The well known Buddhist mantra "om mani peme hung" aims to dissolve, on the vibrational level, the above mentioned states of mind (attachment, anger, desire, pride, jealousy and envy) which, otherwise, keep you trapped in the prison of your ego. You don't need to use mantras, you can as well tune into your spirit and listen to your inner voice guiding you out of the ego-trap of feeling worthless, inferior, guilty, ashamed, damaged in some way, incomplete, needy, and lacking. Your higher self, connected to you via your heart, knows that you are worthy, whole and complete, that your light, your source of love and happiness come from within and cannot be found outside of you. Unconditional love for yourself and others is the feeling expressed by your higher self. Therefore, you always feel worthy of achieving goals coming from your heart. Aiming at targets imposed by the ego and forced by your will might not reflect your sense of worth, and thus that may lead to inner resistance and self-sabotage.

That's why, in case you are not as successful as you wish, it's worth revising your goals in respect to your sense of self-worth first, instead of getting frustrated while trying harder and applying yet another technique to achieve better results.

There is nothing wrong about being wealthy, having a very responsible job, or driving a dream car, as long as this is in alignment with your heart's desire. You have a chance now to recalibrate your goals according to your true innermost wishes and, on the other hand, run a self-check whether you feel worthy of the goals you are currently aiming at.

When you speak from the heart, success will not be defined as a 6-digit bank account, becoming a company CEO, or by the size of a diamond you would like to wear. These notions are secondary descriptions of how you wish your heart's desire should externalize. Your definition of success is primarily a state or a feeling that you know you would like to achieve and internalize. It's a state of happiness, joy, or satisfaction, a feeling of safety and security, respect, love, fulfillment, etc., that you want to become your permanent experience. Once you have achieved it, you would call it success. You might erroneously think, however, that you will reach this state or a feeling first when you enter this house, sit in that car, see the account statement or hug your soul mate. You need to go back to square one and start at the basis—that slight shift in your approach will make all the difference. When you let your inner voice speak first, and then only get a sense of how your success would feel, you will always feel worthy of it because it comes from within. You have a good chance to thrive then. If, however, you rationalize what you need to be successful and make a business plan matching the outcome and not the other way round, you will aim at something that you imposed onto yourself from outside. Your sense of self-worth might not match the rationalized plan and you are prone to end up striving to survive. This explains why techniques telling you to imagine the outcome and try to feel as if you were in the situation work only as long as you stay in alignment with your heart.

Some patterns that overrode your innate worthiness might have biased your sense of worth. Therefore, you might want to take a look at the old beliefs and release them in order to make space for your self-worth to support your success.

When you think of wealth as success, the underlying thought might be "I want to reach a state of financial stability". If it comes from the heart place, it will come from a feeling "I feel worthy of security and I want to provide for my family out of love for them" and it will be in alignment with your heart and, therefore, you will find ways to reach your goal; if however it comes from a place of lack "I want to make sure that we don't end up having not enough", it will be based on fear, which dictates the need of making money. In such a case, your actions will be based on the power of your will, which can carry you far but won't last forever.

Likewise, if you define your success as a leading position, the sponsoring thought may have come from an inner drive to prove something to yourself or your parents, or exercise power and influence, then it will be built around some "should" types of beliefs and will be carried merely by the power of will. If, however, the feeling "I'm worthy of being given responsibilities; I'm worthy of making a difference" will be a driving force, you will work towards your goal in alignment with your innermost wishes and are likely to become very successful. Objects and situations are only outer manifestations of your inner dreams, so if you have a certain picture of success in your head, go backwards to the sponsoring thought and find out if it is fueled by ego and will power, or comes from your heart and is aligned with your true self.

Our heart is our primary organ—it may happen that the brain functions stop but the heart is still beating and the body is still alive; once the heart has stopped beating, brain waves never go on. It starts with the heart and it ends with the heart. The heart feels; it does not rationalize. It is, therefore, the source of information for your intuitive mind, coming from your higher intelligence, your higher self. The most successful people emphasize that it was their inner voice and not their rational mind that brought them that far; their intuition, their "gut feeling" was oftentimes their best advisor. Steven Jobs captured it so accurately, "Your time is limited, so don't waste it living someone else's life. Don't be trapped by dogma—which is living with the results of other people's thinking. Don't let the noise of others' opinions drown out your own inner voice. And most importantly, have the courage to follow your heart and intuition. They somehow already know what you truly want to become. Everything else is secondary."

The rational mind expresses itself in a form of a logically thinking intellect. However, as Einstein said, "The intuitive mind is a sacred gift and the rational mind is a faithful servant. We have created a society that honors the servant and has forgotten the gift" and, he added, "We should take care not to make the intellect our god; it has, of course, powerful muscles, but no personality." Therefore, even if you find yourself to be a rational person used to basing your decisions and plans upon logical conclusions, you have now an opportunity to try a new approach and consult your heart for a change and then check the outcome with your sense of worthiness.

There are three steps for creating a solid basis for your success based on your sense of self-worth. Let's examine them.

Step 1: Become clear what would make you feel successful.

Make a list of everything you associate with success. For instance, you may feel that you will be successful when you have reached satisfaction of having raised children who found their direction in life, when you have obtained security for yourself and your family, made certain type of experiences, managed to cope with specific challenges, obtained certain qualifications, made some spiritual explorations which brought you closer to your inner Light etc. The first step is to get a sense how your success would feel. If you cannot specify the feeling easily, put your hands on your heart, go deep within, and listen to what your inner voice will say. Then speak it out loud. When you hear yourself pronounce your inner wish, you will feel the vibration of it; you will be able to distinguish whether it is your true heart's desire spoken out loud or your ego pronouncing some old patterns of belief.

Step 2: Check whether you feel worthy of it or not. Ask yourself, "Am I worthy of . . .?"

Step 3: It is crucial for your success to treat the answer to the above question seriously and act accordingly:

If the answer is "Yes" and you feel worthy of your self-defined success, then you need to define your success in measurable terms, break it down to manageable steps, make a plan, and go ahead.

If, however, the answer is a "No," and you don't feel worthy of being successful, setting goals would be in vain, as they would fall prey to some self-sabotage pattern based on low sense of self-worth. In such a case, you need to explore this specific area of your life in depth.

Begin with general inquiry: *"What am I worthy of in the area of _____?"* Then ask yourself, *"Why don't I feel worthy of this success?"* and some old beliefs and patterns will surface and become clear. Then, you need to dis-empower them in order to be able to give up the self-sabotaging behavior in that specific area of your life to allow your potential to unleash. You may use the worthiness cards to remind you of what you are worthy of in a visual way, listen to some inspiring webinar, or seek a support of a like-minded group of people in a seminar. You don't need to manage all aspects of your life on your own; you are worthy of support in all areas of life.

When you start facing old beliefs, some may feel odd or even painful. Let them go. Don't judge yourself for having acquired them. You acted to the best of your abilities back then, and now you have a chance to refurbish the old patterns if you find them out-of-date.

I saw once a great saying on a wall of a conference room: "Walk your own path, and let people talk". Have you chosen your path yourself? Or are you listening to what people around you say and define yourself accordingly? Whose life do you live? Yours, or a life planned and designed for you by your family, teachers, bosses, and friends? You are worthy of being yourself after all. Isn't it then the time to start living your own life and break free from the learned "should" and "shouldn't"? Yes, you are worthy of freedom on all levels: not only on the physical one but also on the emotional and mental one. Therefore, it is absolutely all right to free yourself of old beliefs. It might take you some time to get there but if you wish for the transformation, it will take place.

We are a *"No, don't!"* society: We have constructed our reality in such a way that children have to undergo training of what they should not do, in order to be able to survive in our world. What about re-thinking our ways and help children focus on what they could do to thrive in this world instead?

Louise L. Hay, an amazing woman who made a difference in hundreds of thousands lives all over the world as an author and a publisher giving voice to other extraordinary thinkers, arguments why it would be vital to change the focus on what generations are taught right from the beginning: "I have never understood the importance of having children memorize battle dates. It seems like such a waste of mental energy. Instead, we could teach them important subjects such as How the Mind Works, How to Handle Finances, How to Invest Money for Financial Security, How to be a Parent, How to Create Good Relationships, and How to Create and Maintain Self-Esteem and Self-Worth. Can you imagine what a whole generation of adults would be like if they had been taught these subjects in school along with their regular curriculum?"[5]

Since the school system doesn't offer such a life-skills curriculum, you need to make up for it now. Let's have a look at some beliefs and blockages coming from the socially and culturally acclaimed background acquired as you were growing up, but does not serve you any more.

As a child you, too, got your share of:

Don't!
Don't you dare!
Stop! Don't!
You shouldn't!
Don't you ever!
It's not allowed to!
How dare you!
You can't!

As you would hear them, your resistance met those statements, because you felt that they were limiting you in some way. They often stopped you from trying something new, doing things in your own way, living the life you hoped for, taking risks and facing challenges you felt you were able to conquer. Instead, you were constantly downsizing your own image and adjusting your expectations towards coping with life according to the "don't do's" and "can't do's" you were made to follow. You were a child back then, you had to obey in most cases; you are an adult now—you can choose if you still want to live small in some or most areas of your life or if you take the step into your greatness.

I love Marianne Williamson's message "Our Deepest Fear"—let me quote the opening lines which express our human condition, characteristic of the state that most people on this planet dwell in. When I read it for the first time, I couldn't stop tears from rolling—I think it was the first shadow release I have undergone consciously:

> "Our deepest fear is not that we are inadequate. Our deepest fear is that we are powerful beyond measure. It is our light, not our darkness, that most frightens us. We ask ourselves, who am I to be brilliant, gorgeous, handsome, talented and fabulous? Actually, who are you not to be?"

Someone told you once what you were not, what you could not, and should not do. Not being taught otherwise, you started believing it. Now it's time to shake the old beliefs off like a dog shaking raindrops off its fur when returning home on a rainy day. It's time to tell yourself who you really are and what you are worthy of.

Tell yourself now:

I'm worthy of daring
I'm worthy of respect
I'm worthy of being myself
I'm worthy of living my life
I'm worthy of being capable
I'm worthy of trying something new
I'm worthy of living by my own choices
I'm worthy of making my own decisions
I'm worthy of happiness, lightness, fun and joy
I'm worthy of receiving and accepting support and help in life

I'm worthy of _____

I'm worthy of _____

I'm worthy of _____

Now, put an exclamation mark next to the above statements that resonated fully with the new you. There might have been some statements where you still hear the old "Don't!" louder than your own inner voice.

You can add anything that crosses your mind to the above list. You can use the inspirational deck of the worthiness cards accompanying this book to remind yourself on a daily basis of all that you are worthy of. They will help you to keep and strengthen your focus. You can also draw one card a day and make this particular area of your life a focus for a heightened sense of self-worth. You can put the cards up around your house making them into beautiful "road signs" on your new path to healing, which will re-direct your mind to the new course, not letting it wander off back to the old habits.

Let's consciously strengthen your self-esteem by over-writing the old "Don'ts" with the choices based on the feeling of self-worth:

Please complete the sentences with the phrases you used to hear as a child and which are a part of your personal story. Then respond to it from your today's perspective:

Old pattern: "Don't you dare _____."
(Finish the sentence the way you used to be told)

Your response now:

I'm worthy of_____

Old pattern: "Stop! Don't _____."
(Finish the sentence the way you used to be told)

Your response now:

I'm worthy of_____

Old pattern: "Don't you ever _____."
(Finish the sentence the way you used to be told)

Your response now:

I'm worthy of_____

Old pattern: "It's not allowed to _____."
(Finish the sentence the way you used to be told)

Your response now:

I'm worthy of_____

Old pattern: "You shouldn't _____."
(Finish the sentence the way you used to be told)

Your response now:

I'm worthy of _____

Old pattern: "How dare you _____."
(Finish the sentence the way you used to be told)

Your response now:

I'm worthy of _____

Old pattern: "You can't _____."
(Finish the sentence the way you used to be told)

Your response now:

I'm worthy of _____

Old pattern: "_____."
(Add a sentence the way you used to be told)

Your response now:

I'm worthy of _____

Old pattern: "_____."
(Add a sentence the way you used to be told)

Your response now:

I'm worthy of _____

Whenever the old "Do not's" and "Should not's" happen to clang in your ears, make them snooze with longer and longer intervals, introducing the new statements which will help in eliminating that old, negative and untrue influence.

Freeing yourself of the old ballast starts with taking the first step: genuinely invite change. The next step is: stay open to what is unfolding ahead of you, not resisting opportunities just because they seem unknown. And last but not least: take action and actively seize the new possibilities that come your way.

Change is a scary concept for some. I used to be afraid of change myself, associating it negatively with transience and loss. Now I love the notion of change: it gives freedom—it gives you a chance to start anew or try a different approach. Things change, so you can try new things, bring your relationships to a new level, make your life more enjoyable. What a comforting thought, isn't it?

If you feel resistance to a possible change when facing an opportunity of transformation, just consider if it is going to make you happier to stay in the present condition? Please answer the following questions honestly:

Are you leading a life you really want to lead? Are you fulfilled and happy? Are things in their flow and unfolding naturally? Is joy and balance your everyday state of mind? Do you feel safe and secure? Or are some old fears still frequently active in the corner of your mind? Are you looking forward to going to work on Monday or are you counting days till Friday, waiting for yet another weekend? Are you permitting yourself to take time off with ease and without a feeling of guilt? Do you always say "Yes" when you feel like saying Yes and say "No" when you want to say No?

Did you hesitate what to answer or maybe even said "No" a few times? If you did, it might be worth exploring further means of creating a fulfilling life, life interwoven with energy and joy.

Having worked with your worthiness, having answered "What am I worthy of?" question in respect to different areas of your life, you have replaced a number of destructive beliefs, cultivating new thought patterns which will make you stronger and more self-confident. You will not accept certain behaviors any more, be it your own or towards you.

Now it's time to give yourself a gift of yet another method of building up your self-esteem step by step. I will give you two examples at first, leaving a few forms with blanks for you to fill in. For the example I'll take the area of work to give you an idea how you can efficiently go through the process. Following the topic of work, I suggest that you take a look at the areas of love, your family life, health and life-style as well any other topics that you would like to work with.
Example:

What are you worthy of in the area of your _work_?
I am worthy of enjoying my job.

What is your strongest competence in this area?
My strongest competence in the area of my work is my reliability.

What are you most proud of in the field of _work_?
I'm proud of being a good team player.

What is your greatest wish in the field of your _work_?
I wish I were paid better.

Resulting worthiness affirmation:
I feel worthy of being paid well.

What stops you from having your wish fulfilled?
I'm afraid to approach my boss about the salary raise.

Resulting worthiness affirmation:
 I feel worthy of asking.

What is your biggest fear in the field of your _work_ ?
My *biggest fear is that I will be made redundant*.

Resulting worthiness affirmation:
 I feel worthy of security.

What is your biggest weakness in the area of your _work_ ?
My biggest weakness in this field is   that I am not good at follow-up.

Resulting worthiness affirmation:
I feel worthy of admitting weaknesses and asking for support.
What is nurturing you most in the area of your _work_ ?
What is nurturing me/my spirit/my soul at work is having fun with my colleagues.

Resulting worthiness affirmation:
I feel worthy of having fun while doing my job well.

What would you like to experience in your _work_ ?
I would like to receive more recognition.

Resulting worthiness affirmation:
I feel worthy of recognition.

What would you like to achieve in the area your _work_ ?
I would like to become the department manager.

Resulting worthiness affirmation:
I feel worthy of being given responsibility.

Goal: To receive a salary raise, become the department manager and ask for support with follow-up.

How do you plan to achieve the above in the area of your work ?

Action steps (cut your big goals into manageable chunks):

1. *Revise my achievements and areas of competence*

_____

2. *Learn to delegate tasks connected with follow-up*

_____

3. *Consciously allow myself to dare, no matter whether I fail or*

succeed as the result

4. *Make an appointment to talk to the boss about current*

achievements and a possible promotion

5. *Build an additional stream of income to enhance financial*

security

This was an example of how you can work with some issues in the context of self-worth, breaking bigger issues down to smaller chunks that you will be able to cope with more easily.

You can also create helpful affirmations relating to your personal situation. You are worthy of following your dreams. So define your goals and go for them!

Now approach other aspects of your life in a similar way.

Love

Let's have a look at love in the context of your life. Please always remember that no matter who you are and what your life story has been, you are always worthy of love, of receiving love, and of giving love. What is your personal experience of love in your life?

What are you worthy of in the area of <u>love</u>?

I am worthy of _____

What is your strongest competence in the area of <u>love</u>?

My strongest competence in the area of love is _____

_____

What are you most proud of in the field of <u>love</u>?

I'm proud of _____

What is your greatest wish in the field of <u>love</u>?

I wish I _____

Resulting worthiness affirmation:

I _____

What stops you from having your wish fulfilled? _____

_____

Resulting worthiness affirmation:

I _____

What is your biggest fear in the field of <u>love</u>?

My biggest fear is _____

Resulting worthiness affirmation:

I _____

What is your biggest weakness in the area of <u>love</u>?

My biggest weakness in this field is _____

Resulting worthiness affirmation:

I _____

What is nurturing you most in the area of <u>love</u>?

What nurtures me/my spirit/my soul in the area of love is ____

_____

Resulting worthiness affirmation:

I _____

What would you like to experience as far as <u>love</u> is concerned?

I would like to _____

Resulting worthiness affirmation:

I _____

What would you like to achieve in the area of <u>love</u>?

I would like to _____

Resulting worthiness affirmation:

I _____

Goal: _____

_____

How do you plan to achieve the above in the area of <u>love</u>?

Action steps (cut your big goals into manageable chunks):

1. _____

_____

2. _____

_____

3. _____

_____

4. _____

_____

5. _____

_____

Family Life

What are you worthy of in the area of <u>family life</u>?

I am worthy of _____

What is your strongest competence in the area of <u>family life</u>?

My strongest competence in the area of family life is _____

_____

What are you most proud of in the field of <u>family life</u>?

I'm proud of _____

What is your greatest wish in the field of <u>family life</u>?

I wish I _____

Resulting worthiness affirmation:

I _____

What stops you from having your wish fulfilled? _____

_____

Resulting worthiness affirmation:

I _____

What is your biggest fear in the field of <u>family life</u>?

My biggest fear is _____

Resulting worthiness affirmation:

I _____

What is your biggest weakness in the area of <u>family life</u>?

My biggest weakness in this field is _____

Resulting worthiness affirmation:

I _____

What is nurturing you most in the area of <u>family life</u>?

What nurtures me/my spirit/my soul in the area of family life is

_____

Resulting worthiness affirmation:

I _____

What would you like to experience as far as <u>family life</u> is concerned?

I would like to _____

Resulting worthiness affirmation:

I _____

What would you like to achieve in the area of <u>family life</u>?

I would like to _____

Resulting worthiness affirmation:

I _____

Goal: _____

_____

_____

How do you plan to achieve the above in the area of
<u>family life</u>?

Action steps (cut your big goals into manageable chunks):

1. _____

_____

2. _____

_____

3. _____

_____

4. _____

_____

5. _____

_____

Health

What are you worthy of in the area of <u>health</u>?

I am worthy of _____

What is your strongest competence in the area of <u>health</u>?

My strongest competence in the area of health is _____

_____

What are you most proud of in the field of <u>health</u>?

I'm proud of _____

What is your greatest wish in the field of <u>health</u>?

I wish I _____

Resulting worthiness affirmation:

I _____

What stops you from having your wish fulfilled? _____

_____

Resulting worthiness affirmation:

I _____

What is your biggest fear in the field of <u>health</u>?

My biggest fear is _____

Resulting worthiness affirmation:

I _____

What is your biggest weakness in the area of <u>health</u>?

My biggest weakness in this field is _____

Resulting worthiness affirmation:

I _____

What is nurturing you most in the area of <u>health</u>?

What nurtures me/my spirit/my soul in the area of health is

_____

Resulting worthiness affirmation:

I _____

What would you like to experience as far as <u>health</u> is concerned?

I would like to _____

Resulting worthiness affirmation:

I _____

What would you like to achieve in the area of <u>health</u>?

I would like to _____

Resulting worthiness affirmation:

I _____

Goal: _____

_____

_____

How do you plan to achieve the above in the area of <u>health</u>?

Action steps (cut your big goals into manageable chunks):

1. _____

_____

2. _____

_____

3. _____

_____

4. _____

_____

5. _____

_____

Lifestyle

What are you worthy of in the area of <u>lifestyle</u>?

I am worthy of _____

What is your strongest competence in the area of <u>lifestyle</u>?

My strongest competence in the area of lifestyle is _____

_____

What are you most proud of in the field of <u>lifestyle</u>?

I'm proud of _____

What is your greatest wish in the field of <u>lifestyle</u>?

I wish I _____

Resulting worthiness affirmation:

I _____

What stops you from having your wish fulfilled? _____

_____

Resulting worthiness affirmation:

I _____

What is your biggest fear in the field of <u>lifestyle</u>?

My biggest fear is _____

Resulting worthiness affirmation:

I _____

What is your biggest weakness in the area of <u>lifestyle</u>?

My biggest weakness in this field is _____

Resulting worthiness affirmation:

I _____

What is nurturing you most in the area of <u>lifestyle</u>?

What nurtures me/my spirit/my soul in the area of lifestyle is

_____

Resulting worthiness affirmation:

I _____

What would you like to experience as far as <u>lifestyle</u> is concerned?

I would like to _____

Resulting worthiness affirmation:

I _____

What would you like to achieve in the area of <u>lifestyle</u>?

I would like to _____

Resulting worthiness affirmation:

I _____

Goal: _____

_____

_____

How do you plan to achieve the above in the area of
lifestyle?

Action steps (cut your big goals into manageable chunks):

1. _____

_____

2. _____

_____

3. _____

_____

4. _____

_____

5. _____

_____

Please choose any area(s) of your life you would like to "reconstruct", consciously addressing some issues in this specific field, consciously acknowledging your imperfections and weaknesses:

What are you worthy of in the area of _____?

I am worthy of _____

What is your strongest competence in this area?

My strongest competence in this area is _____

_____

What are you most proud of in this area?

I'm proud of _____

What is your greatest wish in this area?

I wish I _____

Resulting worthiness affirmation:

I _____

What stops you from having your wish fulfilled? _____

_____

Resulting worthiness affirmation:

I _____

What is your biggest fear in this area?

My biggest fear is _____

Resulting worthiness affirmation:

I _____

What is your biggest weakness in this area?

My biggest weakness in this area is _____

Resulting worthiness affirmation:

I _____

What is nurturing you most in this area?

What nurtures me/my spirit/my soul in this area is

_____

Resulting worthiness affirmation:

I _____

What would you like to experience as far as _____ is concerned?

I would like to _____

Resulting worthiness affirmation:

I _____

What would you like to achieve in the area of _____?

I would like to _____

Resulting worthiness affirmation:

I _____

Goal: _____

_____

How do you plan to achieve the above in this area?
Action steps (cut your big goals into manageable chunks):

1. _____

   _____

2. _____

   _____

3. _____

   _____

4. _____

   _____

5. _____

   _____

Consider the possibility of accepting yourself the way you are, with all your inner beauty and all your shortcomings that make you a perfect human being. And as the worthy and competent person you are, you can set an intention to let go of your attachment to negative emotions, heal, and grow.

As you are embracing your imperfections, try to feel compassion for yourself and understand that they are the result of past events and actions. Stay non-judgmental: whatever happened, happened. Accept it. Change your script and rewrite your story so you can look forward with positive expectations. Be patient with yourself as long as you stay on the right course. Transformation takes time.

As you are worthy of healing, you know that the present moment brings you an opportunity to realize that you can consciously make a different choice and your life is going to be more fulfilling.

All the fears you speak out loud lose their power piece by piece and, soon, it will be easier for you to look them in the eye. They might still be there and occasionally lift their hissing heads but you will remember that they are just fears that everyone has and that they are not the leading force of your life. When you verbalize a fear, you move it from the emotional to the conceptual level. It is then easier for you to work with it and address the specific aspect directly, instead of responding fearfully to the whole situational context. Little by little you will manage to learn how to get detached from its clenching power.

You know now what areas of our life you would like to change, so that they really reflect what you are worthy of. You also specified your fears. You became aware and made a short action plan of what you can do to transform the current situation into life wisdom, enriching circumstances. It is an amazing awareness! Congratulations!

There is the "dark side" in us, the so-called shadow, and there is the contrary aspect of our nature, the "light" in us. A sound feeling of self-worth and a strong sense of competence resulting in your high self-esteem is like your treasure and is the light aspect of yours. We know that if we embrace all our potential and live our light, our life will be fulfilled. We know that if we follow our inner voice, we will stay true to ourselves and that we will feel good.

If you have followed all the processes, you have re-designed your "house" of self-esteem; you laid solid foundations of self-worth, placed a strong ground floor of competence on it, rebuilt the walls and refurbished the interiors. However, no house can exist without a roof. It is love that tops your house of healthy self-esteem. You are worthy of love; you are worthy of receiving and giving love. And self-love will make you complete as a human being.

The first person waiting for your love is you. You cannot emanate love and love others deeply or even unconditionally until you love yourself.

"So how do you love yourself?" Louise Hay advises, "First of all and most importantly: Cease all criticism of yourself and others. Accept yourself as you are. Praise yourself as much as you can. Criticism breaks down the inner spirit, and praise builds it up. Look into a mirror often and simply say: I LOVE YOU, I REALLY LOVE YOU.

It may be difficult at first, but keep practicing and soon you will mean and feel what you say. Love yourself as much as you can and all of life will mirror this love back to you."

Our culture suggests that your worthiness depends on what you do in life rather than on who you are. But it's who you are that makes a difference: your actions always result from what you think and what you feel; they are the outer reflection of your inner being.

Do you remember who you are in your core? You are a worthy human being. And so is everyone around you without an exception. However, many impersonate learned patterns and live a life of imposed unworthiness. Can you imagine what would happen if every person on Earth knew they were worthy? Can you think of the world inhabited by people conscious of their worthiness, governed by people realizing everyone they are representing is worthy, bringing up children respecting their self-worth? Might sound at first as some utopian idea but it's not because I am talking about the birthright of every human being to live their worthiness from within. If our generation shifts their awareness and becomes fully aware of this intrinsic gift, we will respect and foster the self-worth of the coming generation resulting in a global shift. We, the human race, are worthy of acknowledging who we are.

CHAPTER 9

THE SOURCE OF

YOUR TRUE WORTHINESS

You know you are worthy. However, are you aware of where your sense of worth originates?

You have undergone "The 1 Question Process" and you are able now to specify what you are worthy of in any life situation. It is a very essential tool having the power to raise your awareness and change your life quality when you apply it and act accordingly. It can help you feel more fulfilled. But it will not give you the final sense of satisfaction, completeness and peace as long as you don't realize where your sense of worth is coming from. You will always have a feeling that some piece of the puzzle is missing.

The source of your true worthiness is unshakable and non-negotiable. It is so innate and sacred to your being that once fully realized and experienced, you will never doubt being a worthy human being any more.

The material world will not give you the answer to what your true worthiness is, and what it's based on. Undergoing the process will give you clues about your inner greatness. You will discover more and more about your self-worth until one day your rational mind might step in and say that logically seen, you have reached the limit of what you deserve. "Deserving", "not deserving", "being good enough" etc., are words your ego likes to use. However, your ego is not the source of your worthiness. Your ego is an accumulation of abilities, attitudes, learned behavioral patterns, wounds, accomplishments, failures, emotions and the beliefs based on all the above. Your ego is not a constant in your life—although it is dominating most of the time in most situations, it is changing and dependent on the outer circumstances. Thus your ego is not a source of your inborn sense of self-worth.

Your true worthiness comes from inside—it expresses the greatness of your spirit, the divine spark, higher self, god, the essence, the source, your Buddha nature—choose the word you feel most familiar and comfortable with. Each of these words is just a label for what all people feel inside, although they often cannot name it: it is something greater than your ego, something you know to be the core of your nature. Something you automatically feel respect towards; thus feeling it is an intrinsic part of you, you automatically feel worthy of respect. You feel the innate goodness and kindness in your core; thus knowing it is inseparable of you, you feel worthy of love. You feel it is of a higher quality and wisdom than your daily internal conversations are made of; thus aware that it's the part of you that has the higher knowing, you feel worthy of the connection to the divine.

The source of your worthiness is always present in you. Your task is to stay aware of the part of you that is present beyond your ego. You are conditioned to follow your ego's ways; however you need to know that you can always step back and tune into your spirit to feel your greatness and experience your true worthiness.

There is an interdependent body-mind-spirit triangle; it's helpful to balance the other two to gain an easier access to the inner wisdom of your spirit. It's recommendable to ground your body by having more contact with nature, getting some body work performed on you (for instance massage, acupuncture, general detoxification, etc.), integrating some movement into your daily routine (yoga, pilates, walking, or tai chi etc.), drinking enough water every day, and providing your body with healthy food. On the mind level, you have an ongoing internal dialogue based on the judgments of people, situations, and yourself that your ego is busy issuing. Your constant thoughts crossing your mind can be compared to the noise caused by the tin cans tied to a newlyweds' car. With such a noise around, you wouldn't be able to follow the conversation in the car. Likewise, your constant thoughts and tides of emotions jam the perception of your inner voice. Some thoughts are useful, and some however are automatic and responsive, thus not creative. Some people are flooded by emotions leaving no clear picture, although they color every perceived situation according to the arising feelings. It is helpful to develop a new habit of not following constantly whatever surfaces in your mind. You need to quiet the train of thoughts and calm down the rollercoaster of emotions to start perceiving your inner wisdom clearly. There are ancient as well as contemporary techniques, programs, and methods (among others yoga, meditation, breathing techniques, "A Course In Miracles", shadow work, etc.) that can help you quiet your thoughts and emotions. Stopping the mental chatter and the emotional ride won't result in you becoming a boring person which is an argument of many who believe they will stop enjoying the world as the result of the inner work. What really happens is that you stop being a slave to the automatic reactions and attitudes of your ego, and start discerning between what brings you further or what is merely junk that has simply been allowed by the default mode of your mind. Once you have deactivated the automatic reactions, you can start creating the desired outcome. You are bound to feel more joy and become free to focus on what's really important to you. The more space of mind you experience, the easier it becomes to base your decisions on the voice of your higher self and your innate sense of worthiness—and that leads to inner peace, happiness, and fulfillment.

The outer world constantly expects from you good looks, a smile on your face, politeness, performance, responsibility, actions, involvement, results, and so much more—so you need to drink from the inner well of your true worthiness to stay your authentic self without falling for all the outer demands.

How much more time do you need to allow yourself to feel worthy in every aspect of your life? Are you ready to open up and connect to your spirit, the source of your worthiness? Can you give yourself permission to become your authentic you, independent of the world's opinions of you? It's the right time to claim the best of yourself. Once you have focused on your light, not your shadows, on your strengths, not your weaknesses, on your inner treasures, not the world out there, your life will change.

Give yourself permission to step fully into your worthiness. People usually wait for others to acknowledge them or give them a permission to do something. Seize your personal power now by permitting yourself to live your greatness, shine your light upon others, and share the gift of your uniqueness. Everyone is endowed with many gifts, and even if you do things someone else can do too, you give them your own personal touch and that makes a lot of a difference.

Dare to give the world the gift of you. To sustain clarity and your inner strength in all life circumstances, plunge into your source of worthiness, your spirit—that's one of the greatest gifts you can give yourself. And you are worthy of it.

You are worthy.

Chapter 10

CHANGE YOUR LIFE,

CHANGE THE WORLD

You have been actively changing your life by taking three steps towards unleashing the power of your self-worth: you listened to your inner voice, you consulted your physical wisdom and you worked on different aspects of your life. Each answer you gave was like a gem—accumulated, they constitute a valuable treasure. That gave you solid basis for building a house of strong self-esteem. Afterwards you explored your sense of competence and reminded yourself of all the successes, big and small, that you have achieved throughout your life, which became the walls of your house. You were encouraged to cover the house with a roof of self-love manifesting as your beautiful, inner light. However, the existence of light indicates that there is space with no light, the so-called shadow side of you. You were shown that shadows are nothing to deny or be ashamed of, just an indication of the areas to focus on. Once you are aware of them, they will no longer hold you back; they will no longer be secret rooms in your newly reconstructed house. You were encouraged to plant a flower of self-forgiveness into your garden of life. And finally, you addressed some old *"Do not's!"* and *"Should not's!"* replacing them with a new version of the story of you.

On this journey you have gained an awareness of your worth. It is a treasure that you can use to enhance the quality of your life and secure success—however you define it. Moreover, asking the question, "What am I worthy of?" can help provide insight. Whenever you feel uncomfortable in some situation or you have a choice to make, if you doubt whether you are doing the right thing or, simply, when you want to get some clarity and a direction in life, you can use this question.

Just ask yourself: "What am I worthy of?" And keep asking this question. If possible, speak the first thing that comes to your mind to actually hear the inner answer out loud. It will have a stronger impact than just thinking thoughts.

Have a dialogue with yourself – ask, answer; ask, answer; ask, answer and so on:

"What am I worthy of? I'm worthy of . . ." Just say out loud the first thing that comes to your mind. And ask again: "What am I worthy of?

I'm worthy of _____

and again: "What am I worthy of?

I'm worthy of _____

and again: "What am I worthy of?

I'm worthy of _____

"And in the _____(fill in) aspect of this situation, what am I worthy of?

I'm worthy of _____

And so on till you get clarity and the full picture referring to the situation you are questioning.

Rest assured that your spirit, your inner wisdom, your inner voice—whatever word you use to call your Higher Self, higher consciousness—will speak the truth. And you will know it: it will feel true to you, it will sound true to you, it will feel just right. The next step is—act upon it.

Having worked with your worthiness, having answered the "What am I worthy of?" question in respect to different areas of your life, you had a chance to dissolve a number of destructive beliefs making room for new habits, cultivating new attitudes and enhancing your self-esteem which will make you stronger

143

and more self-confident. You will not accept certain behaviors any more, neither your self-destructive ones, nor others' towards you. Dennis Waitley, a founding director of the National Council of Self-Esteem with a doctorate degree in human behavior, emphasizes, "The most important key to the permanent enhancement of esteem is the practice of positive inner-talk". Reminding yourself again and again of what you are worthy of, not only brings you back to focus but also actively contributes to the strengthening of the core element of your self-esteem. You will start feeling clearer in respect to your intentions and expectations, happier, and more peaceful.

No one can do your push-ups for you. You hold a diamond in your hands: The question that can change your life. You have a choice now: after having finished reading this book, you can just nod your head and put it onto the shelf with a comment "Interesting . . ." ending this journey here. However, if you answered the question as often as you could and worked through the answers and the practical applications and implementations, you will notice a transformation taking place in your life.

Anna, a friend of mine, has done the "1 Question Process" as one of the first people I worked with. She enjoyed the exploration and actively worked with this question again and again. One day she called me, excitedly repeating, "It works, it really works!" and told me what happened at work. Anna is an excellent physiotherapist and a very patient, kind person. Nevertheless, she had a day when she got two very grumpy and disrespectful elderly patients who treated her very impatiently and impolitely, although she was doing her best. Half way through the treatment she could hardly bear it any longer and said to herself: "I am worthy of respect". Nothing changed for a while but she kept focusing on this thought and the feeling of being treated with respect, neither sliding into self-pity or victimhood, nor developing negative feelings towards the patients. After a while the first miracle happened and one of the patients excused himself and explained that he had a sleepless night and pain in his leg all day long which made him very irritable. Little did Anna know that she was up to an even bigger surprise: the other patient who made an impression of hating her work and treating her accordingly, stopped at the door when leaving, turned around hesitantly, and asked in a friendly manner: "Will I see you tomorrow again? You are very professional and I really enjoyed the treatment." It was the power of her focus that made the patients feel it and acknowledge it openly to her, after she had shifted from negative feelings and judgments, towards her true innate feeling of worthiness.

Even though you have completed the exercises, you can apply the question in your life further on, asking yourself again and again "What am I worthy of?" and exploring all the "I'm worthy of _____" possibilities and not agreeing to live anything that does not match the answer. But please remember not to fall for the question: "What do I deserve?" as it might lead you to conventional "should-and-shouldn't" ego-based answers. Instead, listen to your inner voice that will tell you what you are worthy of. It will make a profound difference to the quality of your life, the people around you, and the world out there.

When you recognize what you are worthy of, you give yourself a life-long gift. You will feel, act and react differently. Your life can become now more successful. You know you are worthy of safety, so your choices will be different. You have experienced how good it feels to be worthy of love, respect, healthy choices etc., so you will not be satisfied with anything that doesn't match it any more. As the result, you will create reality based on different standards. You are a part of humanity. You count. Therefore, your thoughts, attitudes, and actions influence others: by raising and broadening your awareness, you contribute to the collective awareness.

Who you are makes a difference. By changing your way of thinking and acting, you impact your surroundings, increasing the awareness that feeling worthy is a birthright of every individual. By changing your life, you change the world. The transformation of your surroundings will induce a change in your community and the ripples of the understanding of worthiness will spread globally. Transforming your attitude towards yourself and discovering your inner treasures, has the effect of you touching the future of the planet. You are a worthy member of the global community of humans.

Humans equal in their feeling of being worthy of love, happiness, health, success, safety etc. At the same time, all are equally worthy to be themselves and live their lives in their own unique ways.

Each of us is worthy of success. But each of us defines success differently. It is all right. Each individual, contributing to setting new horizons and a variety of outcomes, will take a different course of action.

Each of us is worthy of making our own choices. But each of us will make a different choice. And it is good this way. It makes the world an interesting place of diversity.

Everyone is worthy of pursuing his or her goals. But each person will aim at his or her individual targets. It is a perfect approach because only a constellation of all pieces makes our world versatile, interesting, full of possibilities, and worth living in.

By finding out what you are worthy of, you will set an example for your children, your family and your community. You will be able to give the next generation a life-long gift of self-worth, creating an environment for them where their feeling of worthiness will be fostered. You will make a difference in their lives by respecting their self-worth and teaching them by example how to live a meaningful life valuing one's own self-worth.

You have been given an opportunity to get a conscious access to working with your inner world: self-worth and competence resulting in enhanced self-esteem, as well as forgiveness providing you with inner freedom. Using self-worth as a reference point for your success will enable you to live your heart's desire. If you apply it in all areas of your life, you can secure changes that you have been longing for. You will feel worthy of new opportunities and will suddenly notice doors opening where you saw none before. If you only wish to do so, you are now ready to start making a major difference in others' lives: sharing your new understanding, you will change the world around you. Share what you have learnt, experienced and realized. Teaching is the best way of learning. Even when you think you still have a way to go, you can cast light for those who are just entering the path of exploring and unleashing the power of their self-worth. The drops of wisdom which you will share with your surroundings may come down as a rain of transformation in another part of the world as you never know what impact your words have on people and what difference they will make due to your sharing just one question: "What are you worthy of?" You never know how far your influence reaches. My favorite quotation by Henry Adams is: "I touch the future. I teach."

It is my dream that everyone will be given an opportunity to rediscover their sense of self-worth—the inner treasure in single people. If you find this idea worth spreading, share this question with others! There is no guru, no outside person needed to tell you what you are worthy of – you know it yourself. So does everyone. Reconnecting with your self-worth is just one question away: The 1 Question Process that can change your life.

The birthmark of our human race is our worthiness. When we all become aware of it, the global awareness will change. And it will be a change leading every individual to a more fulfilled life. Yes, I have a dream. And you . . .?

REFERENCES

FOOTNOTES

[1] Marshall B. Rosenberg, *Nonviolent Communication: A Language of Life: Create Your Life, Your Relationships, and Your World in Harmony with Your Values*

[2] Marshall B. Rosenberg, *Nonviolent Communication: A Language of Life: Create Your Life, Your Relationships, and Your World in Harmony with Your Values*

[3] Wayne W. Dyer: *Your Sacred Self: Making the Decision to Be Free*

[4] Sonia Choquette: *The Answer Is Simple . . . Love Yourself, Live Your Spirit*!

[5] Louise L. Hay: *You Can Heal Your Life*

APPENDIX

HOW TO USE THIS BOOK

This book is primarily meant to be your manual guiding you to unleashing the power of your self-worth and securing you more happiness, love, understanding, inner freedom and an overall fulfillment in your everyday life.

You are welcome to take it as a reference and initiate transformation in your surrounding. Once you have done the exercises, you can take it one step further and bring it you to your friends and your community. Share what you have learnt, experienced and realized. Teaching is the best way of learning. Even when you think you still have a way to go, you can cast light for those who are just entering the path of exploring and unleashing the power of their self-worth. The drops of wisdom which you will share with your surroundings may come down as a rain of transformation in another part of the world—you never know what impact and difference you can make just by sharing this one question with others: "What are you worthy of?"

You can initiate a group of people to meet a few times in a row to explore self-worth together. Everyone has got the sense of his or her self-worth. Many are not used to think about themselves as worthy but everyone can connect to this inborn human quality easily once shown the way. You don't need a big guru or some advanced technology to make you aware of your worthiness. Anyone who has been through this exploration and applies the principle of questioning oneself "What am I worthy of?" is able to guide others on this journey that, in turn, will guide others in the future. It is a grass root movement of spreading the consciousness of your innermost value that you build a meaningful and successful life on.

Here are some practical tips how to run such a meeting:

The group shall be facilitated by a person who has already been through the "1 Question Process", be it by reading this book, attending a webinar or a seminar. It is vital that the location chosen for the meeting shall provide privacy so that people can unfold and speak freely without being disturbed or worrying that someone in the next room would follow the conversation or loud music next door would invade your working space. Feeling of security and privacy is the basis for a successful unfolding. Hence, it is important that all the members of the group feel that whatever is said will stay in the circle.

Set the time frame, so that people know what to expect. Start the meeting on time by setting an intention that everyone may benefit from the process. Then start the round by everyone reminding each other what they are worthy of in general, asking the "What are you worthy of?" question. One person asks the question again and again, letting the other person reply with one statement "I'm worthy of..."

Important: the person asking the question does not validate, judge, or prompt the answer, their role is solely to provide the space where the other person can explore their sense of self-worth. The person whose turn it is to answer says, "I'm worthy of . . ." using one word or a short phrase, not adding any story to it, no explanation or justification.

You can make it a group or pair work, depending on the size of the group, whatever feels more comfortable to the participants. Then decide what 2-3 areas of life you will focus on, either according to the order in the book or to some participants' needs. Let the whole group participate, one by one, in pairs or as a group, always depending on the size of the group.

As the concluding part, make a short round where everyone gets a turn to share shortly what they have discovered new and how it will change their life.

If you do it consequently enough, you will witness miracles of transformation of a community. It is your real contribution to changing the world, a ripple that will spread far, followed by many others, turning into waves of change. Enjoy being a part of it!

INSPIRATIONAL RESOURCES

You have explored and unleashed the power of your self-worth. If you wish to go more in-depth into different aspects of your life then I would like to recommend some resources to you that I have found helpful myself:

Books:

Sonia Choquette: Your Heart's Desire
Jack Canfield: The Success Principles
Marianne Williamson: Return To Love
Hale Dwoskin: The Sedona Method
Sandra Ingerman: How To Heal Toxic Thoughts
Deb Sandella: Releasing Your Inner Magician

Online:

Sonia Choquette - Unleashing the power of your spirit and becoming the authentic you: www.SoniaChoquette.com

Lauri DeJulian - Transformational shadow work and dissolving inner blocks: www.KingdomOfMySoul.com

Ella Doron - Valuable self-esteem and self-worth enhancing songs for educational programs for children and teenagers - author and performer: www.EllaVsMountain.com

Byron Katie - The Work: www.thework.com

Shawne Duperon - An inspirational tool for practical application of forgiveness: a documentary film, a DVD and a series of books (release date TBA): www.facebook.com/ProjectForgive

ABOUT THE AUTHOR

MONIKA LASCHKOLNIG

Monika Laschkolnig is an educator, teacher, and a businesswoman currently leading a pedagogical organization with over 6,000 students in Austria, Europe. She has been trained internationally; studied Methodology of Teaching at the English Philology (M.A.) in Poland, as well as Philosophy and Theory of Perception (B.A.) in India, and is a certified 6-Sensory Practitioner, having graduated a series of extensive trainings in the U.S.A. and the U.K., teaching now how to live in connection with your inner wisdom to become your authentic self, and unleash your full potential.

Along with her husband, Martin Laschkolnig, a professional speaker and entrepreneur, she is an Austrian representative of the International Council For Self-Esteem.

Monika holds seminars and teaches workshops internationally on discovering the power of self-worth as the basis of every success. She teaches how to experientially distinguish inner guidance of your higher self from the voice of your ego; as well as how to integrate intuition in all areas of life.

Her interests are diverse and connected to developing human potential on all levels. She is interested in the workings of the human mind and uses an empirical approach to bring theories into practice. She believes that every child is born worthy, intelligent, and is a language genius; that it's imperative to foster these innate abilities at the early childhood stage because if not addressed, they may wither away. Fostering self-worth, self-esteem and supporting the uniqueness of each individual, from childhood through adulthood, is her passion.

Monika lives in Austria, Europe, with her husband and their two children who are growing up with the gift of being raised trilingual and in awareness of being worthy as their birthmark.

For more information about Monika Laschkolnig and her work please visit her website at: www.WhatAreYouWorthyOf.com

MONIKA LASCHKOLNIG

"WHAT ARE YOU WORTHY OF" CARD DECK

Continue the journey with a deck of 72 beautifully illustrated "Worthiness Cards". The "What Are You Worthy Of" card deck serves as your daily inspiration, bringing you back to the worthiness thoughts. The cards will help you to keep and strengthen your focus. Simply draw one card a day and make this area of your life a focus for a heightened sense of self-worth. You can even put some of the cards up around your house making them into beautiful road signs on your new path to healing and unfolding, which will re-direct your mind to the new course, not letting it wander off back to the old habits.

I'M WORTHY OF

HAPPINESS

I'M WORTHY OF

LOVING MYSELF

I'M WORTHY OF

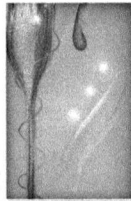

LEADING A FULFILLED LIFE

Make use of this great tool to remind yourself of all that you are worthy of on the daily basis. To order, please visit us online ...

www.WhatAreYouWorthyOf.com